This sacred text belongs to:

If found, kindly contact me here:

This book is dedicated to my husband, Paul, who's my loudest and most passionate cheerleader, to our fur babe, Lucy, who's been my comforter through thick and thin, and to our magical little girl, Audriana, who is the greatest healer, honor and refiner of my life.

Thank you for choosing (and changing) me.

Welcome, kindred spirit...

It was a balmy, midsummer afternoon. I curled over a small corner table in a near-empty sushi restaurant, picking at my salmon roll and nursing a mug of green tea. The sun poured in from a tall block of windows, washing over my bare shoulders, as though inviting me to join it.

A gush of cold air from a floor vent wafted over my feet. I fidgeted in my chair, avoiding my friend's gaze, wanting only to disappear into a pile of blankets and pillows in my bed at home.

From the outside looking in, I had a world of reasons to be excited about my future: I was young and healthy, had a fun and flexible job, and was enrolled at a university that nurtured my aspirations in progressive ways. I'd been invited to spend the day gliding across the lake under the hot sun with a group of friends. Instead, I was practically anesthetized by sadness-far too fragile to be amongst the bare skin and laughter and splashing and shrieks.

I'd found myself staring into the eyeballs of a level of sorrow I never dreamt I'd meet-the kind that had a cold and unrelenting grip around my sense of self, and was slowly strangling my future.

Most mornings, forcing my body from bed and pressing my feet against the carpet felt like slinging cement. I'd been in a relationship for years that was akin to being trapped inside of a mental dungeon-one that had become so indescribably possessive and violating and emotionally paralyzing, my family feared I'd never find my way out of its dark and twisted maze.

He treated me like property, as though he were the architect of my life, and, for reasons I couldn't explain, I let myself believe him. Somewhere in the midst of the chaos, I became convinced that I was the keeper of his happiness and the cause of his eruptions and degradations. I became an equal participant in the dysfunction and the cat-and-mouse game. I forgot how to advocate for myself, how to trust myself and how to know myself.

Yet, the truth had always been this: the relationship was merely a symptom of a scarier problem: I didn't love myself. I was oblivious to my value and was searching for it in so many lonely places I'd never find it.

During those days, I'd lock eyes with my reflection in the mirror and hurl incredibly scathing digs my own way—feeling livid with my weak-mindedness, while haunted by the hiss of childhood grief and trauma I'd never had the courage or tools to completely unpack.

I wanted to soar across big, open landscapes. I wanted to marvel at wondrous things and spark meaningful conversations. Near completing my degree, I ached to give volume to the beauty and ugliness inside of me, and to illuminate the human experience in vivacious ways. I wanted to be the kind of writer and journalist who painted with broad, colorful strokes. I wanted to enliven and reveal and soothe. And I wanted to anchor peace, purpose and serendipity into my orbit. I felt as though I was flunking Earth—padlocked inside of a cage of my own creation, depriving my dreams of the oxygen of self-belief.

Yet, somewhere in the midst of so much depression and shame, somewhere deep inside of me, something tugged at my self-doubt and whispered into my consciousness, flashing with the possibility of better days. It called to me with authority, reminding me that my mother had not panted and waddled through nine long and sweaty, sacrificial months of growing my bones and eyelashes and organs for me to waste my potential away and suffocate under a spell of manipulation and misery.

It was time to admit to myself that there'd always been an element of choice, no matter the misfortunes that had landed in my life. I'd been turning my nose up at opportunities that asked to empower and rescue me. I'd chosen to stay in that awful, mind-numbing loop; no one else ever had the dominion to choose it for me.

Somewhere in the belly of my despair, I got so fed up with my low-level beliefs, shipwrecked decisions and wasteful inaction. I'd grown tired of sucking at life. I thought, "I don't know how to crawl out of this hole, but I'm going to challenge everything I think I know for sure..."

I began nodding "yes" to experiences that made me recoil with resistance and shiver with vulnerability. I started to follow the fragrance of my curiosities, and to let myself be guided by a sense of wonder. By morning, I'd take the long route to class or work, filling my car with lectures and podcasts that injected me with the prospect of a brighter world. By night, I'd lounge in bed with one book after another in my hand, devouring anything that lit up my heart and throat-punched me with fascination and intrigue.

I signed up for mission trips that shattered my privileged delusions—traipsing along dirt paths and wandering through ancient ruins with dozens of humans I'd never met. I let myself be transported by the teachings of Bruce Lipton and Napoleon Hill, and comforted by the wisdom of Maya Angelou and James Baldwin. I put my nose to the carpet and prayed. And I flung open doorways of surrender so that divine insight and providence could come pouring in.

About a year later, I stood inside of a radically different life. I had the same brain, the same feet, the same childhood memories and the same genetic blueprint, yet I was the steward of a new consciousness–one with a garden of seeds that were blossoming with promise. The only thing that had really, truly changed was my mind. And, because of that, the world in which I lived held an entirely different shape and vibrated with a more vivid tone.

Fresh possibilities and a renewed zest for life came gliding onto the scene. Hope and resources flickered where I'd only seen storm clouds before. I held my degree in hand and stamped the soul-sucking relationship with its long-overdue expiration date. I began to breathe freely. I felt my wings stretch out.

Not long after, I met and fell in love with the man who would become my husband. About five or six years after that, I was writing for top magazines and media sources. And, today, I've got a multi-faceted career as a mental health and relationships journalist, essayist and editor, and I'm a mom to a little girl with the sweetest disposition. She's so magical, some nights I struggle to pull my eyes away from the baby monitor because I love her so much.

I live inside of a movie that feels as though it were dreamt up by a considerably more kind and gracious screenwriter. Because it was. Which, my dear kindred, is precisely what this book is about.

You may have read my words in publications like Oprah.com, *Oprah Daily* (formerly *O, the Oprah Magazine), Marie Claire, POPSUGAR* or *Cosmopolitan*, or heard me as a guest on podcasts like *Earn Your Happy* or *Minding the Mental Mess* with Dr. Caroline Leaf.

Over the years, I've had the luxury of working with some of the most eminent psychologists, neuroscientists, self-made entrepreneurs and spiritual thought leaders of our modern day, including Dr. Deepak Chopra, Daymond John, Gabrielle Bernstein, Dr. Shefali Tsabary, Dr. Venus Nicolino, Dr. Judy Ho, Julia Cameron and many others.

I've strolled through their minds and been sparked by their expertise. I've researched the disorders and dysfunctions they treat, and the healing modalities and success strategies they've championed. I've studied the psychology of love and grief and prosperity and connection and intimacy.

I've made the human quest for personal renovation and fulfillment my playground of discovery and understanding. And I'm madly in love with the brilliantly plastic organ that is your brain, and, most specifically, how much freedom you have to anchor its power and reroute your path through the world. Few topics are as enthralling to me. My goal is that, by the time you bow out of this experience, you'll have fallen in love with it and be inspired to further explore its power, too.

But, before we begin, I need you to be open to this: if something called or stirred or winked at you to purchase this program, even if on impulse, you might consider that it wasn't an accident. I believe this material was meant to find you. And you were meant to find it. Your more beautiful and empowered life is excited to welcome you with applause and high-kicks. Perhaps it's been chanting and cheering for your arrival. You get to decide whether or not you'll step into it.

The following pages are assembled in an actionable, digestible format, and broken down into four strategic phases:

Phase I: Purge
Phase II: Reimagine
Phase III: Let the Light and Wonder in
Phase IV: Build a Beautiful Future

Because this program is all about you, you get to choose your timeline. I've broken it down into three possible paths:

Path One - one phase each week, making it a 28-day program, which is doable for many, but aggressive.
Path Two - one phase every two-week period, which is the most popular and by far the one I most recommend, making it an eight-week program.
Path Three - at your own scheduled pace, which is fine so long as you commit to staying on course, following the progression and crossing the finish line.

I'll be walking with you all the while, pointing you toward a more confident, enchanted and resolute version of yourself. Some of the exercises and tasks might sucker-punch you with motivation and joy, while some won't feel fun at all. Some will require a focused stretch of reflection, and you might find yourself spending three days on a single one, whereas others present only a short, thought-provoking story. I structured it this way intentionally, as to avoid overwhelm.

All I ask is that you show up with an open spirit and make a vow to your own freedom, healing, fulfillment and success, whatever that means for you.

Before I swing open these doors, I wish to mention an event that's been extraordinarily defining for me. In fact, it's the precise event that thundered through the trajectory of my entire life, sending me on a treasure hunt toward the reconceptualization of my own grief, pain, healing and personal power, and inspiring my life's work: the tragic, family-wide gas explosion that expired the lives of my mother, my paternal grandmother and my two aunts when I was 6 years old.

One of my aunts was only 20 years old when she died, leaving behind an infant daughter—my cousin. She would've celebrated her 56th birthday today, at the time of this writing. My mention of this is more than a reverent nod to the late women in my family, and it's more than a reflection of the sad hollows I've traveled; it's a reminder that, while they're no longer able to kiss their loved ones goodnight, and no longer have the luxury of editing their legacies, I do. And every pair of eyes colliding with this message does as well.

Which is also to say that this is my holy, official invitation to you to become more alive through this process. Radically. Gratefully. Curiously. Vividly. Responsibly. Joyfully. Compassionately. Powerfully.

If you take nothing else from my work, please take this all the way in: you're far more powerful than you've ever given yourself credit for, but you can't access any of that power if you don't embrace it and take radical ownership of it.

I recently interviewed Dr. Edith Eger for an *Oprah Daily* story {1}. She's a holocaust survivor who became an acclaimed psychologist and *New York Times* bestselling author, and she emits so much supernatural wisdom, it's unbelievable. During the call, while chatting about the nuances of having a romantic mindset and the dangers of living for the love and affection of another person, she said, "No one should ever put their life in someone else's hands. There is no freedom without responsibility..."

If we don't take responsibility for the lives that we've been given, we will exist in chains. We will forever be imprisoned by the betrayals and wrongdoings of others, and the misguided choices of the past that may have harmed or humiliated us. Responsibility means, "I can't change what happened, but I have the choice to be the most awake, compassionate and hopeful steward of this moment." It means asking, "Who do I want to be in this situation—in this day, in this life, in this pain?" Who you choose to be today will inevitably stack another brick in your tomorrow. Which is also to say that your renovation begins with radical responsibility. And responsibility begins with the belief that you have the authority to build a more desirable outcome.

So, then, who's this program meant for?

Who's the person that possessed me to curl over my laptop for months—combing through my vault of expert interviews and scientific data and studies, and thumbing through the weathered, coffee-stained pages of my decade-old journal entries in order to create this material from a place of authenticity and heart?

I'll tell you who.

Radical Life Renovation

This program is for anyone who's ever had their heart or spirit broken.

It's for those who've doubted themselves for way too long-who feel like there's this champion inside of them, dying to come out swinging, but can't figure out how to unlock the marvelous entity from their cells and push it out into the world.

It's for the ones who are tired of watching others do extraordinary things when they *know* they've got potential for their own magic-making.

It's for those who've felt like they can't get it right-whatever "it" is, and are ready to believe in themselves so that they can build a delicious life packed full of enriching connections and contributions and stories.

This book is for dreamers who are ready to become doers. Victims who are ready to become victors. Enemies of self who are ready to become their own best friend.

This book, I believe, is for you.

Welcome to *your* beautiful, new beginning!

YOU'RE HEREBY AT RISK OF THE FOLLOWING:

- Spontaneous jolts of epiphany.
- Creative downloads while in line at the grocery store.
- The sudden nerve to apply, audition, inquire or enroll.
- Late-night experiments that make you shimmy in your pajamas.
- Realizing that you're no longer bothered by that person or enslaved by that opinion.
- A desire to reinvent the wheel.
- Inexplicable surges of hope and possibility.
- Mystical strokes of genius.
- Full-body giddiness and laughter.
- Startling belief in yourself.

You + Me.
It's about to get radical.

Heads up, love! Before you step inside...

I created this program in an effort to provide educational information on a myriad of topics as a public service, which shouldn't be construed as clinical, financial or wellness advice. Though I'm an experienced journalist who prides herself on accuracy and evidence, the following advice is a collection of my personal opinions, observations and perspectives.

I'm in no way your personal adviser, coach or counselor. I'm not a licensed mental health or medical professional.This information isn't a substitute for therapy or professional guidance. It's meant to help you identify and unlock revelations that you might bring to your coach, doctor or therapist, as needed. Always consult a professional in the area of your particular circumstances prior to making any life-altering decisions. Additionally, I may recommend various books and services, but no such reference is intended to be an endorsement that such information is current. **I empower you to always conduct your own research.**

I'd also like to add that, while the majority of my readers are women, I realize not all of you are. So, while I might refer to you as "she" or "her," please use whatever applies to you.

Please know that I know I'm imperfectly human. As excellent as I strive to be in my work, there might be a random typo or evidence of a brain lapse, mostly because, for some chapters, I'm writing with a toddler tumbling over me. I also reserve the right to evolve beyond the ideas presented here. While I know that this program can change your life in profound ways, please understand that I'm continuously changing, too. A joyful and prosperous life doesn't burden itself with the demand for perfection or a fixed mindset. This book is meant to be a heartfelt testament of that ethos.

Lastly, I hope that you'll receive these pages as your companion and sanctuary throughout this process. And, while I've created spaces for you to move through the exercises, and unload confessions, sparks and to-do's, I highly recommend keeping an additional journal handy, should an exercise require lengthier exploration.

Thank you so much for trusting me with your time. In our hyper-digital age, where data is being hurled at you from a million directions, I realize you've got lots of enticing options out there. Your decision to trust me with your precious hours and money is an honor I don't take lightly. I appreciate you. **You're the reason I do what I do.** And my intention is that it's some of the best money you've ever spent.

With all my love, light and power,

Lacey Johnson

PHASE I: PURGE

The time has come to purge the poison from your head, your heart and your environment. Gone are the days of giving emotional, mental, physical or spiritual bandwidth to the things that keep you sick or make you shrink.

Those long-held deceptions are no longer protecting you; they're only protecting what they know. Let's begin by identifying the friends from the foes.

Might there be vast treasures inside of you, hidden under layers of crummy beliefs and tired, old ideas, longing to amaze and shimmer gorgeously in the sunlight?

In a world of whine-drenched commiseration, might we stop venting and start toasting to the things that are going right?

You've got no more reason to hold onto anything that reeks of misery or monotony. From coffee mugs to old love letters, show them the exit door.

Time to stop rattling those chains and step into freedom. Only you have the power to do it.

Whoever someone said you were once upon a time was never the gospel. No one's opinions, good or bad, are your gospel.

If you don't get what you want in the tiny ways, how can you expect to get what you want in the big, shiny ways?

PHASE II: REIMAGINE

There are gifts on the other side of every misfortune. A stroke of luck on the other side of every failure. A rebirth after every death. Here's where you'll shift back into your power and reimagine the truth and wonders of what it means to be you.

Forgiveness isn't rewriting history or glossing over a wrongdoing. It's self-love at its finest.

There's a magic lesson behind every closed curtain. A rejection asking to point you in your next right direction. But only if you've got the self-belief to receive it.

She'd already failed at her first dream, so she thought she'd give another one a shot. A multi-million dollar brand later, she isn't sorry she did.

There's no need to set any part of your history on fire. You don't have to hate who you were in order to get on board with who you're becoming.

Your taste buds are about to satiate the part of you that might be starving most.

The champion isn't always the one who starts off in the lead, but the one who shuffles on when their skeptics are busy snoozing with overconfidence.

You've got one fragile, gorgeous life. One masterpiece to write. If you knew it were the end, what would you wish you'd have said or done differently?

PHASE III: LET THE LIGHT & WONDER IN

Now that you've combed through your expired beliefs and reimagined your truth, it's time to welcome courage, delight and possibility to the party, and to reconvene with the magic that's *always* been inside of you.

PHASE IV: BUILD A BEAUTIFUL FUTURE

The time has come to welcome the miracles. You're going to get those wishes and desires off of your vision board and into your reality. You're going to consciously design a life you'll never have to apologize for, hide from or second-guess.

Ever felt as though you were flunking Earth? As though you just couldn't get it right? If so, leap into a spirit of urgency. It's an elixir of miracles.

The one thing every dying person wants you to know? Run toward your dreams while you can. Live the truth of who you are and what you love, before it's too late.

I heard it straight from a legend's mouth: "I've never made anybody successful. People can only ever make themselves successful."

If you wish to direct the future in your favor, feed your brain empowering ideas, impressions and solutions, every single day.

You've got a divine appointment with your future self–the one who knows all of your next right moves. Ask the master anything... anything at all.

Built to size, magnificently designed and generously adorned to fit your deepest desires, gifts, quirks, skills, talents and personality traits. Yours; No one else's.

You know that person you've always dreamt of becoming? Here you are.

table of contents

The Radical Daily 4

The following are **four transformative tools** you'll be engaging with daily throughout your renovation. These tools spark happiness, rejuvenation and self-connection. Show up for them; they'll unlock magic for you.

1. Morning Mind Reset: In order to retrieve your sense of possibility and power, you need to find it. This means releasing the noisy toddlers from your headspace in order for the voice of wisdom to be heard. Each morning, set a timer for 10 minutes, then unload whatever streams of consciousness come. Don't try to perform or fill a certain number of pages; just release. Whatever drifts to the fore naturally, get it out of you and onto the page.

2. Morning Magnetizing: This is a quick visualization exercise that only requires about five minutes of your time. Shut your eyes, get still and quiet and visualize your face inside of a powerful magnet. Begin to "pull" the things you desire into the magnet. It might be fancy contracts, serendipitous connections, gut laughter, romantic moments, life-changing books, overseas travels, chance encounters, health cures or money-making solutions.

3. End-of-Day Gratitude Bath: Unload a quick list of things you're grateful for that happened that day. It might be two things or 10 things. Whatever they are, bathe in them.

Some examples: the stranger who flashed you a sunny smile while in line at the supermarket. The manicurist who complimented your hair. The co-worker who kindly dropped a latte and a bagel at your desk. The amber sunset. The hysterically precious thing your child said. The challenging deal you closed. The personal record you broke. Whether unforgettable and metamorphic or sweet and small, reflect upon it and soak in its splendor.

4. Nightly Reward Ritual: This is an act of kindness that you're going to give to yourself at the end of each day. It should land like a hug. Some inspirations: Brew a cup of tea and drizzle it with honey. Warm a towel and run a hot, bubbly bath. Spread fresh sheets across your bed. Curl up with an indulgent novel. Light a candle and put on a beautiful piece of music. Slide into a pair of satin pajamas. Bang around on a piano. Find a window seat and relish the sights and sounds of wind or rain or traveling cars. Arrange a bowl of dark chocolate and berries. Go for a sweaty, cathartic run. Stretch across a yoga mat.

Complete each of these daily, with unabashed pleasure. The relationship you have with yourself is the longest earthly one you'll ever have, and it's the only one that's guaranteed. This is a thoughtful path toward repairing and empowering that relationship.

"YOU HAVE TO GO
THE WAY
YOUR BLOOD BEATS.
IF YOU DON'T LIVE THE
ONLY LIFE YOU HAVE,
YOU WON'T LIVE
SOME OTHER LIFE;
YOU WON'T LIVE
ANY LIFE AT ALL."

-JAMES BALDWIN
THE VILLAGE VOICE, 1984

PHASE ONE

PURGE:

to rid yourself of an undesirable
condition, feeling, illusion or quality;

to expel, evict, sweep or wash away;

to become free from what is completed,
disproven, expired or no longer useful.

OPENING EXERCISE:

EXILING THE LIES

They're not protecting you;
They're only protecting what they know...

The gates of renovation have parted. As we prepare to break ground together, I ask that you lay your judgments and reservations to the side, because this exercise, while not the most fun-loving or thrilling part of this program, has the potential to reset the climate of your life. It holds the power to revolutionize your outlook, your self-image and your relationships, and generate surprising, liberating breakthroughs beyond your most ambitious dreams. It's the essential first step. Don't be afraid of it.

Before we begin, I ask that you carve out an hour or two of time, if not more. Silence your phone and slide it into a drawer. Close your laptop and step away from the social media stage. No roommates, no parents and no spouses are allowed. If you're a mom, you might summon someone to watch your child. Because anything or anyone that might muffle the voice of what's begging to be heard is strictly unauthorized to participate in the gift you're about to give to yourself.

Retreat to a comfortable, serene space. You might place a stack of pillows behind your back or toss a plush throw blanket over your lap. Turn on a beautiful piece of music. Pour a hot cup of coffee or a glass of wine if that'll help you unravel. Take a deep, soulful breath. Drop your shoulders. Relax your jaw. Shut your eyes. Know that all is well. With an open spirit, begin to give volume to the choir of chatterboxes in your brain. Hear out the loud-mouths first and get their snarky opinions onto the page. Then wander all the way into the cobwebbed corners, where decades-old figments of disappointment, rejection, shame or unworthiness might slither and seethe in the shadows.

You know the ones. When your life is a blur of to-do lists or is whistling with favor, you don't always know they're there. But, just when you feel brave enough to break out of your cocoon, and launch the campaign, enroll in the webinar, tell the bamboozling lover to take their manipulations where the sun doesn't shine, or have coffee with the hot guy or girl from the library, they start hissing at you, causing you to rethink, or, worst of all, cancel.

There's a simple explanation for why this kind of thing keeps happening, even if breaking the cycle doesn't feel like a stroll through the park: your subconscious mind thinks it's protecting you, but it's only protecting what it knows.

The subconscious mind is the habitual, non-thinking mind that runs the show about 95 percent of the time. It's a record of all of your best and worst experiences, learned skills and observations, stacked inside of a filing cabinet in your brain. In response to those experiences and observations, it laminated beliefs about who you are, the kind of world you live in and the totality of what's possible within it. So, when it demands that you cancel or ghost on something that you truly want, it's going to war with your conscious mind, which is your smarter, more creative and solution-oriented mind that houses your dreamiest wishes and desires.

The negative beliefs stored in your subconscious mind are quick to draw their weapons. They fight to confirm what's impossible, shouting things like, "It's not like you deserve it anyway..." or "Who are you kidding? You're not qualified for this. This is just another one of your silly pipe dreams..." or "You're not like her. You don't have an entourage of friends and family supporting you and you never will...." or "You'll always be unhealthy and miserable and in pain. You're just going to have to learn to live this way..."

These monsters are the ones that'll send each of your most heavenly aspirations straight to their death bed. They don't come from a holy place of intuition, but are downloads from outside sources. Most of these downloads happened during your early childhood years, when your brain spent most of its time in a state called "theta," which is the same brainwave state a person is in when they're under hypnosis or meditating {2}.

Do you realize what this means? Children under the age of 7 are running around, playing with their dolls or trucks, climbing trees and hanging from monkey bars in a near-permanent state of hypnosis. Which means they're super vulnerable to suggestion, and are constantly being programmed by everything they experience, overhear and witness. This is what was going on when you were small, and because you hadn't yet developed analytical skills, you might've been programmed by messages that sentenced you to a life of hustling for worthiness, perfectionism, low self-esteem, scarcity, shame or timidness-sometimes from people who had no idea they were harming you. Because maybe they were acting out of the perfectionistic or timid ideas that were lamented in their subconscious, too.

If you absorb nothing else from this chapter, please take this all the way in: Those deceptions that you may've downloaded and have since accommodated for God-knows-how-long? Those bullying ideas that you've schmoozed and entertained? The internal babbling that keeps on bruising your confidence? They aren't your friends and they aren't doing you any favors, no matter how familiar they might sound when playing on a loop.

Which is also to say that it's time to exile those troublemakers, and show them who's the keeper of your mental castle from now on. If you don't decontaminate your internal environment, nothing will ever improve in the world you walk around in every day. Ever.

So, on the next five pages, unload every doom-filled belief, insult and worry that arises for the following five areas of your life: health and vitality, money, career and success, love and relationships, purpose and spirituality. Invite them to crawl from their dusty crevices and have a candid conversation with you. You've got no more time to cower in fear of them. Your mind is your show to run; not theirs.

This process might seem ridiculous at first, but can quickly become overwhelming because you might be horrified to come face-to-face with the cruel and shameless company you've been befriending in your mind. But these beliefs shove your highest potential into hiding, and they need to be faced, disarmed and kicked out onto the pavement, once and for all. They don't deserve you.

Take as much time as you need, letting the emotions and thoughts drift through you as they may, without judgment. Once you've stared every monster in its eyeballs, return to each page. With a fresh gaze, act as your own confidante and supporter when reconsidering each belief. Then, ask yourself, "Who created this wretched idea for me?"

Perhaps it originated from the overcautious parents who made you fearful and skittish of harmless things. Or, perhaps, parents who were broken and troubled, and subsequently passed down their broken and troubled ideas to you. The stuffy first-grade teacher who never smiled. A bully on the school bus with pepper in his teeth. A messy ex-lover who wore the same underwear for three straight days. A catty, insecure co-worker who caught her thrills from shooting down anyone's ideas that didn't accentuate her own.

Next, ask yourself, "Is this belief realistic? Is it sane? Do I respect the source who planted its seed? Have I been believing something that's laughable? Outrageous? Might I dispute this idea with powerful evidence to the contrary?"

I know from experience: an absolute lie, when believed, can rip through your life and damage you at every turn, as though it's the absolute truth–even if it's not rooted in a fraction of truth. So, expose the lies and confront their poisonous messages. Face what you've been blindly obeying. Once you determine every belief that's meritless (some will seem straight-up revolting once drawn to light), disempower each by crafting a new, life-giving mantra in its place–one that's grounded in bravery, intuition, possibility and your highest potential.

Like, for example, "This is just another one of your stupid pipe dreams..." might be rewritten as "This dream has endured inside of me for years. It's alive and well and stomping around for good reason, and I've got what it takes to champion it. By building an educated plan that's fueled by bold, consistent action, I'm already on my way to realizing it. It's not a matter of if, but when..."

Or, let's say you're stuck in a belief that you're incapable of attracting friends who clap and cheer when you shine. You might rewrite that self-sabotaging lie as, "In the past, I gave my energy to people who didn't have my back, but I'm learning that the more I love and support myself, and the more I affirm my own worth, the more I attract people who mirror it back to me. So, from here on out, I release anyone who isn't sincere, and I invite only those with good intentions to stick around."

Some of your new truths will feel fraudulent at first. Your default will absolutely be to reject them. And, when so, know that it's your highly efficient brain, fighting like mad to hang onto its stubborn neural pathways {3}. But, while your brain might be a skilled salesman at convincing you that it's protecting you from scary intrusions, which is sort of beautiful when you think about it, just remember that it's only protecting what it knows.

If you want to transform your life, you must feed your mind new information on a consistent basis, much in the way that you learned your ABC's, or shapes and colors, or how to tie your shoe laces, and can now recite or perform tasks in and around that knowledge without even thinking about it. This is because repetition is king.

So, consider this exercise a bold announcement to that brilliantly plastic organ of yours that, starting today, you're going to exterminate the mental dust mites and demons. As you purge, you're going to replace them with dazzling new guests-ones that toast to your individuality, joy, luck, wealth and well-being. Ones that are kind and gracious and wise.

While it's true that everyone's brain plasticity declines with age, aside from cases of severe traumatic injury or degenerative diseases, the process is ongoing until you die. This means your brain never loses the ability to rewire and reorganize itself; it simply requires an engine of desire, attention and repetition. Which means you've got the powerful opportunity, beginning now, to redesign your mind. And, thus, your life.

You can make breathable, accommodating space for new truths. You can give them light and care and uplifting conversation. You can invite them into the most private rooms of your heart and psyche. Daily. With time, they'll become permanent residents who'll never dream of leaving. Remember: you're no longer a child being programmed by your caregivers. You're calling the shots from now on. No matter how much toxic stress, criticism or pessimism you may've been exposed to during your early development {4}, or anytime since, and no matter what disempowering beliefs you were sentenced to, you're now an adult who stands in authority. You govern your mental kingdom. You're the director of who and what you entertain, engage with and feed.

Your time and space are your own. You've got the power of choice, and you get to declare the lies from the truth, and the foes from the friends, today and forevermore.

EXILING THE LIES

HEALTH & VITALITY

THE LIES:

MY NEW AND ABUNDANT TRUTH STATEMENT:

EXILING THE LIES

MONEY

THE LIES:

MY NEW AND ABUNDANT TRUTH STATEMENT:

EXILING THE LIES

CAREER & SUCCESS

THE LIES:

MY NEW AND ABUNDANT TRUTH STATEMENT:

EXILING THE LIES

LOVE & RELATIONSHIPS

THE LIES:

MY NEW AND ABUNDANT TRUTH STATEMENT:

EXILING THE LIES

PURPOSE & SPIRITUALITY

THE LIES:

MY NEW AND ABUNDANT TRUTH STATEMENT:

BEDTIME STORY:
THE GOLDEN BUDDHA

What hidden treasures have you got buried inside of you, longing to gleam gorgeously in the sunlight?

It was the 1950s in the heart of Southeast Asia. Amongst the tropical beaches and swaying palms and opulent royal palaces, a group of young monks rallied together in a circle at a temple in Thailand, following instruction from their superiors to relocate a 10-and-a-half-foot Buddha statue that had been stored on the property for hundreds of years. It was made of clay and covered in splatters of filth-never one to be shown much veneration, as far as they knew.

In the midst of the move, one of the monks noticed a tiny chip in the clay. Beneath it, a speckle of gold shimmered strangely in the sunlight. *What could this be?* he wondered. Intrigued, he grabbed a hammer and a chisel, and began gently applying pressure around the chip, assigning himself to the task of finding what else lurked beneath.

By nightfall, the monk gaped in amazement at the sight that towered before him. The statue, though long believed to be made of solid clay, was, in fact, made of solid gold. It had merely been covered in clay. As word spread across the temple, a flurry of other monks rushed toward the statue, surrounding it in astonishment. They couldn't believe their eyes. How had this treasure been kept in the dark for so many generations?

Legend has it that, several hundred years before this discovery, a group of monks covered the statue with clay, in preparation for a brutal attack by the Burmese army. But, when the attack pillaged through the monastery, those monks were killed, along with the truth of the Golden Buddha. This meant that every living soul that succeeded the attack would believe the statue was nothing more than what could be seen from its murky exterior.

This was until the glorious truth was revealed-one that's said to currently be valued at almost $200 million dollars.

This story has been passed around for years, though I'm unsure of its original source. Regardless, the takeaway is clear: What if there's an undiscovered world tucked behind what the eye can see?

Which brings me back to you.

As you drift to dreams tonight, I want you to spend 10 minutes or so meditating on an idea: What if your golden potential has been hiding under layers of filthy beliefs for years or decades-dying to astonish and glisten gorgeously in the sunlight?

Perhaps the shame stories you tell yourself each time you reach for a higher salary. The stomach-turning humiliations that you replay in your head, convincing you that you're awkward or second-rate or unworthy of being heard. The guilt and regretful procrastinations you've been schlepping around for years. What if those icky layers of emotional and mental residue have been concealing the most priceless-and most true-parts of you?

Returning to the belief-examining exercise in the previous chapter, are there any further lies that pop up and come slithering to the fore? Any other filthy deceptions that you've been unnecessarily accepting as the truth about who you are and what you're capable of-perhaps ones that are secretly housing a goldmine?

What if you've got brilliant adventures, conversations and inventions tucked away inside, longing to gleam courageously in the open world, and bless so many lives, including your own, if only you'd be brave and curious and stubborn enough to chip away at the ugliness covering it all?

Goodnight, treasure-seeker. I've given you a lot to think about. Let's reconnect when you're ready to go even deeper.

PHASE ONE

PURGE

MIDPHASE
LOVE NOTE:

Every day, that big, beautiful brain of yours fires more than 6,000 thoughts. This means, in a 24-hour window, you've got more than 6,000 chances to either affirm and encourage yourself, or twist your mind and nervous system into an anxious spiral.

That's over 6,000 shots at entertaining an idea that could potentially restore your health, or revolutionize your relationships, or multiply your bank account balance.

That's more than 6,000 times to remember what you're made of, to envision a kinder outcome, and to revise the holy masterpiece that is your incomparably special, mega-eventful, definitely-not-an-accident life.

BEDTIME STORY:

MY LIFE IS INCOMPLETE... WITHOUT SOMETHING TO COMPLAIN ABOUT?

In a world of whine-drenched commiseration, cancel culture and juicy gossip, how often do you talk about what's going right?

About a decade ago, while waiting for my name to be called at the doctor's office, I was flipping through magazines when I stumbled upon a fascinating article featuring a CEO of a Fortune 500 company who'd entered into an experiment with a psychologist. In it, he'd committed himself to eliminate all negative talk for 30 days.

If he found himself being baited into an argument or tempted with an irritation, he'd pause, drop his shoulders, unclench his jaw and make a note of it. At the end of each day, for a month, he was to document any compelling observations he'd made.

By the 30th day, his reports were astonishing, both professionally and personally. He cited stunning transformations in nearly every area of his life-including his attitude when he awoke in the morning, the ways in which he interacted with his team and his nightly exchanges with his kids about their sports activities and grades.

Suddenly, his employees were no longer ducking out of conference rooms to avoid him, but were approaching him with fresh ideas and strategies. They were even (gasp!) looking him in the eye.

After reading it, I was both intrigued and supercharged with inspiration, and decided to create a mini-experiment of my own. For an entire week, I'd neither criticize nor complain, no matter how many bullies I encountered or how much doom-filled news I overheard. This meant no fiery expletives while navigating traffic. No chiming in when a friend spewed a catty remark about someone we mutually disliked. No calling myself a "stupid idiot" when I dropped my wine glass on the hardwood.

Well. Let it be known that this was an illuminating experience, to put it delicately. Mostly because I found that, the majority of time, I no longer had anything to say. I'd hear my phone buzz, but could only gaze helplessly in its direction. What was I supposed to say to the person who was eager to unload every tumultuous detail of their latest romantic predicament, or rant about their tyrant of a boss for the 100th time?

As the days dragged on, I was shocked by how many educated and resourceful people relied on their limitations and offenses as fuel, and how often I witnessed someone's sky-high expectations crash to the ground. I found that, for the most extreme offenders, it was as though their life was incomplete without something to complain about. They handled their problems like priceless treasures they'd be lost without, and used their venting episodes as a means to bond with the ones they loved.

But, most disturbingly? I was stone-cold guilty of those self-destructive habits, too. So many of my conversations were unconsciously toxic. And, I realized that, each time I highlighted my personal dramas and called upon my rolodex of limitations, I was keeping myself trapped in situations I could have so easily wiggled free from. This realization was life-changing for me, and it planted seeds of self-awareness and responsibility-ones I continue to call upon whenever I need to give myself some tough-love and spank my thoughts back into a more grateful zone. (Which is always.)

Many years later, when my daughter was a newborn, I briefly reconnected with a former co-worker. We'd both held a fondness for each other-once sharing laughs and swapping romantic fiascos during work breaks. As it often happens, our lives had taken dramatically different paths in the years since. At the time, mine had become a blur of breastfeeding, diaper changes and writing deadlines, and couch hangs with my husband, baby and dog. I'd come to mostly live in leggings, even while working, and felt like a straight-up goddess on the rare occasion that I curled my hair. I wasn't exactly society's picture of cool anymore, but I was in love with it.

Hers looked a bit different-seldom void of an adrenaline rush. She was never without a nefarious story to unveil. When we worked together, she was often leaping in and out of relationships, moving apartments, and untangling herself from one fiasco in order to entangle with another. "I'm a glutton for punishment, I guess, but it makes for lots of funny stories," she'd once said, with a wink. In those days, I admired her unfettered ways. She was exciting and free, in my eyes. But, after reconnecting, I realized that, while little had changed for her, a lot had changed for me.

One night, shortly after reconnecting, she asked to speak by phone, saying she wanted to run something past me. I agreed to chat after I put my baby to bed. For the first few minutes, we traveled through the usual banter that you exchange with someone you haven't talked to in ages. It was light and nice. But, before long, I found myself turning my mouth away from the phone, muffling yawns, realizing that she'd done nothing but unpack one theatrical quandary after the next.

Anytime I steered the conversation in a positive direction, she'd grab the spotlight back and shine it over the many devils she'd been battling. It was hysterical. Also disturbing.

At the time of this writing, I come to you almost two years into a global pandemic, a fragile economy, frustrating supply shortages and a historic level of mental health struggles. More than five million people have died worldwide-a harrowing number that's grown forcefully {5}. There've been months at a time where hospitals were so overwhelmed that patients were wheeled into cafeterias and gift shops for urgent treatment [6}.

I've got close friends who've lost so heartbreakingly much-from a beloved parent who they were unable to be with during the final weeks of their life, to the thriving business they poured all of their creative and monetary resources into for years. Add to that a historic level of political divisiveness and vitriol and violence that's ripped through America as of late. It's been a wild card of an event to live through, digest and witness. The truth is, so many people have a nightmarish story to tell, and definitely plenty to complain about.

In my own life, I've seen and danced with some awful, gut-wrenching things over the years. At 6 years old, I watched the building that housed my family's furniture store business burn 10 feet away from me, not knowing if both of my parents were inside-later learning that, though my dad had been spared, my mother and three other family members hadn't been. And, in the aftermath, there were months at a time when I couldn't go a day without witnessing an adult in my life curled into a chair, weeping desperately. It was a time of loud silences and endless questions. There were never not saturated tissues scattered about.

And, beyond that early childhood experience, there have been countless other conundrums and griefs and heartbreaks in and around my life and that of close family member's-from abusive relationships to post-traumatic triggers to religious turmoil to a series of medical nightmares to unexplained infertility.

But nothing about my life's narrative is special. Humans are often inclined to compare circumstances and say things like, "Wow, she had it rough," or "Yeah, but you've had it pretty easy, so be grateful." But that kind of thinking thrives in the absence of empathy and truth, and it's dishonoring to what a person might be moving through. Nearly every human on this planet, even the ones that might appear to be disgustingly lucky and problem-free, almost certainly have a vault of stories that haunt them.

Perhaps they've been mistreated, neglected or short-changed. People they trusted who abandoned or violated them in horrific ways. Opportunities they deserved and strived for endlessly, but failed to realize. Yet, no matter what's happened or what is to happen, I know this: no one heals and nothing progresses if everyone broods, criticizes and rants their life away. Because, while losses and traumas should be acknowledged and processed, and injustices should absolutely be exposed and reformed, making a spirit of gossip, self-pity or vengeance the centerpiece of your conversations will never serve you or the world.

The way you communicate matters tremendously in terms of your mental and emotional health; the profound success of neuro-linguistic programming therapy (a language-based intervention that seeks to help a person see their problems from a new perspective) confirms this {7}.

Now, before I go on, please don't misunderstand me. My stance isn't in promotion of toxic positivity, nor do I believe in minimizing a cruelty or prejudice that's shown up. Not ever. But I do believe this: so many of the crushing things that may happen to you will not at all be your fault, they won't be fair, and you won't have deserved them, but the way you respond to each of them will always be your responsibility. This in non-negotiable. And it's also freeing. Because that's how you discover solutions. That's how you take back the reins of your life and return to your power.

How you use your energy and where you steer your mind will inevitably co-create the kind of movie you'll live in. Every time. It's not the event that happens to you that creates your life; it's the event combined with your response to it that makes your reality what it is.

I fidgeted impatiently as my former co-worker cantillated about her string of misfortunes and vendettas. And, while she probably thought I'd find her dramatic tales to be riveting and juicy, and that I was on the edge of my seat, foaming at the mouth for more, the truth is that I found them to be extraordinarily boring. I couldn't wait to end the call, crawl into a bath and scrub away the images she'd just projected onto my brain. And I haven't taken a call from her since.

I care about her and wish only the best for her, of course, but I've got no interest in her drama. Because, while her life has no scarcity of action, her story never moves. The cast members and sets may change periodically, but there's no talk of self-reflection or action toward forgiveness and resolution. And I find that to be a total snooze.

I imagine how, if only she'd channel her unbridled charisma and fun-loving irreverence toward enlivening conversations and activism, how much beauty and providence she might create for herself and others. Most importantly, how much more empowered and happy she'd feel. Because, in a world where rant culture has become fashionable, it's not cool. Scientists have long determined that chronic complaining is poisonous to both our mental and physical health {8}, and I think we can all agree that there's nothing cool or interesting about unnecessarily poisoning ourselves.

While your existence alone is fascinating, your drama isn't. In fact, it's boring and it sucks. While it might make for some rollicking entertainment for a season or so, eventually, it'll make a huge yawn of your life. It'll never take you closer to your most cherished goals-the ones you absolutely deserve to realize, especially after everything you've been through.

A couple of years ago, I interviewed Gabby Bernstein, *New York Times* bestselling author of *Super Attractor* and a slew of other celebrated books, for an *O, the Oprah Magazine* (now *Oprah Daily*) story about managing jealousy in friendships {9}. When asked her advice about navigating a friend's negativity, she said something so intrinsically lovely.

Bernstein said, "Many of my students ask me how to maintain their high vibes when the people around them are stuck in negativity. My response is, 'Always carry a flashlight.' It serves as a constant reminder of your ability to shine light, even around the darkness of others."

So, as you lay your head on your pillow tonight, I invite you to consider something:

How often do you stew about what's going wrong? Like, say, the obnoxious neighbor who parks too close to your mailbox. The overbearing friend who's notorious for interrupting. The annoying in-law with expectations that make you groan. The lack of sales on any given day, or the incompetent barista who frothed the wrong milk before your big meeting.

And, finally, steep on this: How often do you talk about solutions? Wins? Possibilities? Light-filled alternatives? The people who truly love you?

How often do you chat about what's going *right*?

RADICAL ACTION:

ATONE YOUR ENVIRONMENT

...because there's no reason to hang onto anything that reeks of misery or monotony.

The first celebrity I interviewed for a magazine assignment was fashion designer Betsey Johnson. It was for a feature in *Mirabella*, and I was admittedly geeked out about it. A celebrated icon for more than 50 years, she's dressed leggy supermodels for runways during Fashion Week, styled A-list celebrities for red carpets and magazine spreads, and decked out countless girls for their Sweet 16 birthday parties and senior proms. Her flamboyant designs and playful cherry-print fabrics have long scoffed at societal norms and trends, almost winking with a spirit of rebellious freedom.

Working with her was a delight-not only because her dresses and jackets were splattered throughout my closets since middle school, following me from home to college and to multiple abodes in the years after, but because talking to her was like a breath of fresh, liberating air. It felt like I'd been given a V.I.P. pass to show up as my most brazen, quirky, peacock-like self. Even cooler, she dropped a token of wisdom in our interview that I'll probably never stop replaying in my head, especially when I get dressed in the morning.

She said, "I've always wanted my designs to support the idea of being punk, being pretty or being whatever you want, but mostly about enjoying the process of getting dressed and entertaining yourself and liking what you see. That's what it's all about. For example, I don't own a pair of solid black shoes because I want to look down at my feet and enjoy what I have on them."

I think Betsey is onto something.

We are emotional, energetic, visually-stimulated beings. Studies show that our homes aren't merely places where we eat, bathe and crash. In fact, we're influenced by our environments in consequential ways {10}. Our surroundings either inspire or restrict our creative flow, and either stifle our confidence or magnify its charms.

This might explain why a sun-drenched ocean view whisks you into the arms of serenity. Or, perhaps, why a stretch of snowcapped mountains injects you with a craving for adventure. Also why a spunky change to your hair color might cause you to meander about flirtatiously. (My husband once told me, "Baby, anytime you get your hair done, you act prissy and walk around differently." So, if this one resonates, I get you.)

It could explain why a fragrant floral centerpiece on your breakfast table adds a feeling of spring to your kitchen on overcast days. Why slipping into a pair of silk pajamas makes you feel feminine and sensual. Also why the sight of dirty plates piled in your sink might make you feel frenzied and grumpy-even angry. You get the picture.

The point is, when your closets are so cluttered that you can't find a flattering pair of jeans, your mind is going to mirror that madness. And, when you're stockpiling items in any shelf or room of your home that reek of soured love, misery or monotony, perhaps serving as totems of heartache, regret or restriction, even if from an era of your life that feels like it was aeons ago, it's probably casting a shadow over your sense of freedom and self-expression.

If so, it doesn't have to be this way. You can afford yourself the luxury of glancing around your home and soaking up the scenery with gladness. The colors and scents and textures should bring a smile to your lips. After a long, hair-yanking day spent staring at a computer screen or running after children, you deserve the safety and richness of collapsing into your favorite chair or pillow with a heavenly sigh.

You deserve to experience all of those wonderful feelings. You deserve to wake up and drift to dreams in a haven. So, why rob yourself of that?

Now, listen, before we lean further into this exercise, and you start tossing out half of your possessions, I want to be clear about the intention here. This isn't me bending your arm in a spirit of haste or irresponsibility, nor am I pressuring you to spend money you don't have. This exercise is simply a caring, supportive invitation for you to get transparent with yourself about how you're being influenced by your surroundings, and to then consciously and joyfully build and style an environment that harmonizes with your constitution.

The research shows that, when you strip stale, lifeless or grimy energy from your living space, you stop unnecessarily torturing yourself in small ways that can generate massive benefits over time. Then, you can gradually begin to fill your bedroom or studio or workspace with art and furniture that energizes, soothes and uplifts you. Keepsakes that remind you that you're loved. Post-its that embolden your goals. Handbags that makes you feel like a boss.

So, one by one, I want you to stroll through every room, closet, nook and vanity of your home. Comb through every cabinet and drawer, noticing anything that conjures dispiriting feelings. No pressure to have a certain reaction; just let the energy announce itself.

Some examples: The obnoxious earrings that were a gift from an ex. The outdated coffee mugs overcrowding your kitchen shelves. The boots you wore on the day you bombed the interview of your dreams.

The miserable pencil skirt you snagged on a whim after a crabby acquaintance made a sneering comment about your knees. Maybe even the awards or trophies that make you cringe because, even though you earned them fairly, you dreaded every audition, practice or game along the way, and they now serve as emblems of the years you exhausted yourself for a dream that was never yours.

Interpret this activity however you wish, but be allegiant to this rule: if an item makes your heart ache, your throat tighten or your power shrink, it's got to be hauled away.

Remember: there's no reason to hang onto anything that yanks you into a cave of negativity-whether it be an end table, an old birthday card or a torturous pair of heels. In fact, there's no reason to hang onto anything that doesn't, at least in some facet, enliven and support the future you're in the process of building.

If your environment serves as a showroom of blasé, regretful or traumatic moments in time, or clothes that've never justifiably hugged your curves, your mental state will absolutely reflect that.

Which is also to say that, if your home is adorned with colorful drapery, eccentric art and intriguing sculptures, or piles of soothing blankets, trails of candles and affirming mantras, or luxurious wine glasses, glamorous coffee table books and velvety upholstery, or whatever life-giving mood you're after, your mental landscape will reflect that as well.

Most importantly, remember that this act of purging goes deeper than your home.

You're not merely clearing out your book shelves, kitchen cabinets and wardrobe; you're creating fresh, inviting space within the closets and rooms of your mind. The kind that signals to your neurons to start firing differently. The kind that will then, over time, reinforce those new neural pathways with a sense of accomplishment, celebration, freedom and pleasure, thereby rolling out the red carpet for increased confidence, inspired direction and rip-roaring possibility.

And that's how the magic and the miracles have a chance to come pouring in.

ATONEMENT STRATEGY, PART I

FROM COFFEE MUGS TO KEEPSAKES, AND BEYOND, THESE ARE ITEMS THAT MIGHT NEED TO GO:

ATONEMENT STRATEGY, PART II

BEDTIME STORY:

DON'T BE A HOSTAGE TO WHAT YOU'LL NEVER CHANGE

...because "what might have been" is a dream we pitch to ourselves to avoid beginning again.

So often we spend years of our lives burrowed inside of a mental dungeon, hanging out with ghosts of the past. Rattling the chains of yesterday's mistakes. Beating ourselves up. Trying to purify the poisonous relationship for the 100th time.

If you can relate–if you find yourself a hostage to something that feels frustratingly impossible, or if you're tired of listening to the regretful hiss of bad decisions from long ago, you're going to be liberated by this chapter. The time has come to free yourself.

Ahead are five power-thieving habits to abolish and purge, forevermore. Because your wonderfully bright and spacious future is begging for the chance to be built.

1 Trying to Satisfy the Impossible-to-Please

You know the breed. They're the kind who'll ask you to drive 80 miles at midnight to rescue them from standing in the rain. And, somehow, you feel obligated to do it. You may have left them cheerful surprises on their windshield or dropped soup at their door when they were sick with a miserable flu. Perhaps you've raced out of restaurants, abandoning your fresh pour of wine, warm dinner rolls and charming conversation, in order to listen to them sob inconsolably about yet another disaster.

Sometimes loving them feels like a labor. And it's seldom reciprocal.

When you're giving them everything they want, they might shower you with exaltation and gratitude. But, that shower of love and thankfulness usually becomes a storm cloud before long. Time and again, you find yourself with your nose shoved into a corner or your butt pressed against the hot seat. And God only knows what your punishment will be this time.

The pendulum might swing from glorification to villainization, over and over again, without end. No matter how cheerfully you tiptoed around their expectations or rolled out the red carpet to please them, you find yourself in flames. Maybe you didn't call or text often enough, or didn't sweep up their messes swiftly enough, or didn't martyr yourself hard enough.

You might wonder, Are my efforts ever going to be worth all of the guilt and madness and back-breaking effort? Are they ever going to appreciate me? Is this circus ever going to end?

The answer is no. You're in a dead-end endeavor because their chronic unhappiness has never been about you, babe. You could color all of their skies a brilliant blue and name constellations after them, and crack every bone in your body trying to rehabilitate their problems, but it probably wouldn't be enough for long. Because they'll just create a fresh pile of troubles for you to shuffle through. Chronically discontent people are tortured by an internal raucous that you don't have the power to remedy.

Have compassion for them and send them love. But, please, stop sacrificing your sense of peace for someone who's wired to seek fault and offense. They'll find yet another reason to be disappointed, even in a bountiful garden of charity, kindness and possibility. Stop thinking that being a 'good person' means suffering in silence for others. It doesn't. If you can let them go, release them from your orbit. If you're not in a position to do that, then let the desire to please them go. Because, until they decide to heal themselves, you never will.

2 Romanticizing the Almost-Perfect Relationship That Got Away

When I was 19 years old, I fell euphorically in love with a guy I'd later plan to marry. There was no question if he was "the one." Of course he was, and the feeling was mutual. He often said, "Sometimes I have tears in my eyes because I love you so much." For more than a year, he attached his last name to the end of mine in the most tender of ways. We fantasized about our unborn children. Sometimes we fell asleep on blankets underneath the stars, dreaming of the day we'd make the world our personal playground.

But time tossed us a plot twist, as it often does. As we shed our adolescent wonder and stepped into adulthood, it became clear that the futures we envisioned for ourselves were painfully different. His mother's shock of a cancer diagnosis only magnified those differences. We couldn't deny that our love story was on its death bed. When the relationship flatlined, I feared I'd never love that way again. I spent the decade that followed in a maze of messy romantic entanglements, all the while glancing backward and glossing over the incompatibilities with my first love.

Many times we tried to reenter one another's life and rekindle our belief in forever, both holding a flame for the other that fought like hell not to burn out. But, every time we tried, we succumbed to our non-negotiable differences-in our beliefs, priorities and interests. We still stared at each other with stars in our eyes, but there was no way around the truth without betraying ourselves.

It seemed so divinely cruel-that my life's grandest love story had already been written to reveal a tragic ending. That I would never again love so effortlessly and intensely. But, as it turns out, I was wrong about that.

In the years after our final goodbye, my ex, barely in his 30s, sadly passed away from a year-long health crisis. And, less than two years after that, I met and fell madly in love with the man who's now my husband. While, I might always carry a flicker of tenderness for my first love, the chemistry and connection I have with my husband is far deeper, more enduring and intimate. We share a beautiful life filled with culinary shenanigans and ceaseless one-liners and dreamy travels and heartfelt conversations. And, most significantly, a magical, sassy little girl we named Audriana. We aren't the picture of perfection, because that doesn't exist, but he's "the one" for me, no doubt. I don't want to imagine being guided through a frenzied crowd by anyone's hand but his.

So, if your precious relationship fell apart, it doesn't mean it wasn't meant to be. Maybe it just wasn't meant to be forever. Maybe it already fulfilled a divine and necessary purpose. Let yourself grieve, then do the hard and healing work to let it go. There might be something better that's dying to race toward you and take your breath away. And, in case you didn't already know, allow me to confirm something for you: No matter what's happened, your heart deserves to love again.

3 The Awful Thing You Did That You Can't Forget

I once ran over a dog in my parents' neighborhood, right in front of the owner and his toddler-age daughter. The dog hadn't been on a leash and I'd seen no way to dodge him. When I jerked my car over to the side of the street and let my window down, shaken and tearing with remorse, the owner, obviously panicked and heartsick, launched into me furiously, tossing the dog's bloody remains in my face.

I sobbed into my steering wheel in horror. And then into my pillow for weeks. I could barely look at my car because it had become a carriage of terror and confirmation of what a heinous degenerate I was. For months, I was imprisoned by guilt anytime I remembered it, mourning for that family, letting the nightmare loop in my mind. I chastised myself often, even though I'd never determined how it could've been avoided.

To this day, almost two decades later, I still shiver at the memory of it. But I've forgiven myself because my present and future needed me to. Replaying the scene in my mind never accomplished anything other than further mental torture. There's never been any way to rewind and rewrite a different outcome. And, though I still send love and peace to the family when I recall the nightmarish scene, I can do nothing to prevent the dog from harm. And I can't erase it from their minds either, though I badly wish I could.

So, whatever terrible thing you may've done in your life, remember that you can't change the outcome now. Don't make yourself a hostage to a past transgression. Feel and express your remorse, and fold the lesson into your future, but don't assign yourself to a life of penance. That's so unnecessary. You're already forgiven, if you're willing to be.

4 The Fear of Falling On Your Face

If ever you're brave enough to reach for something that doesn't exist in your present reality, be prepared to fall on your face. You might even take a bloody nose-dive a few of times. I certainly have. The life of a magazine journalist and editor has been interesting, but certainly not all daisies and gold medals and high-fives. I've had stretches of success so exhilarating, I could almost hear the angels singing. But I've also slammed into walls of disregard, rejection and cancelled projects. I've ridden exalting highs and I've tumbled into dirt-kicking lows.

Yet I've always lived to tell, remembering that I'm only bruised and sore because I was climbing toward the thing that makes me come the most alive, and that invites others to come alive. Every reach has been worth the risk of a blow. So, in your life, you're going to stumble and fall no matter what you reach for, so you might as well fall in the name of love.

Fall reaching for what harmonizes with your heart's cry. Fall reaching for what's most enlivening and meaningful and true. How could you ever regret it?

5 The Household Name You Might've Been

If only you'd taken that fancy job after graduating college. If only you'd relocated to that thriving metropolis. Or had the guts to sign up or audition. Or hadn't given that parasite of a person another chance to worm their way back into your heart again. Maybe then, you think, you'd be living out your golden reality in the South of France right now. You fantasize and romanticize all of the things you could've had, or done, or been. Yeah? Trust me, I get it. But hear me out.

None of those potential outcomes exist and never will. "What might have been" is a dream we love to pitch to ourselves to avoid beginning again. It's the lazy way out. You're just putting your life on snooze, over and over again.

Replaying and wallowing in the opportunities you didn't take or might have had only swallows precious time you could spend investing in your future-whether it feels like your second chance or your 100th. The "what might have been" mindset, albeit dazzling, is a work of fiction and always will be.

But, your future? It's wagging wildly in your face, rivaling against doubt, asking that your creative juices surge through the present. It's practically gurgling with anticipation at the chance to be written.

Here's the catch, though: you've got to stop being a hostage to what you'll never have the power to change. Like, ever. You've got to nix the slothful stewing and wake up to what's possible right now. You've got to choose today and tomorrow over the past, forevermore. Because it's all you have to work with anymore. It's all there is. It's all there ever will be.

And, most importantly, you've got to have the audacity and the courage and the gusto to begin... again.

BEDTIME STORY:

STOP HEXING YOURSELF WITH WHO YOU NEVER WERE

...because none of the labels you've been assigned have ever been your gospel.

I was born into a close-knit, conservative, Southern American family. Hot plates passed around the table every Sunday after church. Prayers spoken before bed. Bibles drawn from the book shelf every time a storm blew through. Curse words strictly forbidden. Rules of modesty uncompromisingly enforced. Also droves of care and love.

But, from the time I exited my mother's womb and landed in the big, open world, I began to formulate my own ideas about how I'd engage with it. About what my limitations were. And those ideas and limitations were sometimes different from that of my elders.

While faith and prayer have never not been centric and sacred parts of my life, I wasn't the type of child to curtsy gracefully into indoctrination for the sake of being obedient. I hungered for diverse experiences that challenged the norm. I ached to explore unfamiliar terrain-to taste and touch and feel the pulse of life outside of my bubble, even at the risk of being burned. There was always an itch begging to be scratched. Always butterflies dancing in my belly, asking to fly.

By the age of 15, I practically had a Phd. in pushing boundaries and turning my nose up at the status quo.

As a result, I became known in my family as being a rebel-the one who was bold, unconventional and mostly unwilling to comply. And that label has taken me decades to shed in the minds of some of my loved ones. And, look, if you were to stroll through a showroom of what life was like in my home when I was a teenager, you might agree that the label was fitting. I often stressed my parents into a frenzy with my iron will and razor-edged refusal to never be defined or controlled.

But "the rebel"? That was never exactly it. In reality, my rebelliousness was a manifestation of my curiosities and need for freedom and understanding shoving its way to the fore. I was trying to breathe and form my own opinions. It was as though my brain was shouting, "Wait! What they're teaching me right now doesn't make sense! I have questions!" and "Wait! I'm expected to believe this simply because an older human told me it's the only way?" and "Wait! Is this my life or theirs?"

And, throughout those days, I was fumbling with a blur of macro- and micro-traumas, having found myself at 6 years old living a life I no longer recognized. Wondering why my mom was no longer around to smooth out the wrinkles in my dresses and pack my lunches for school. I was teeming with abandonment and confusion, and desperate to be comforted in a specific way. I was in a dance of suppression and grief. I was afraid of what might happen next. All of these elements spilled over into my perceived "rebellion."

But none of it meant I was innately bad or wrong. Rebellion was merely my battle cry for independence and relief from pain.

Being misunderstood often feels like screaming at the top of your lungs while watching a blur of faces shuffle past you. Adults who're overstressed and saturated in grief might be giving everything they've got to provide care and love, while unaware of the torment a child might be wrestling with. It's common for an adult to assume that a child is too young to understand the depth of a tragic event.

In my case, I understood enough to feel as though I were limping through life with fractured emotional legs. I knew I was being pitied and whispered about at school. And I was desperate to protect my autonomy. I didn't know how to be anything but a free and hungry spirit, nor did I want to find out.

But, here comes the prevailing part: the personality traits that once caused some of my family members to judge me and prayerfully whisper about me with eyes lowered have, at least for the most part, come to serve me victoriously well as an adult-as a writer and journalist and entrepreneur, and as a friend, wife and mother.

My boldness and defiance have allowed me to wander into wonderfully unconventional opportunities. Which is also to say that, any undesirable label I may have been pinned with once upon a time? Those monkeys aren't about me and never were. They've never been anything but someone's perception of me, funneled through the lens of their own dysfunctional stuff. None of those monkeys are mine to carry, invalidate or tame. And neither are yours.

In life, it's as though we lock ourselves into a boxing ring of identification. Some of our labels are our opponents and some are masks we wear. We might throw a punch at a label that's been forced upon us, trying with all of our might to knock it out and dispel its power, once and for all. Or, we might dodge the punches life hurls our way, desperate to protect a label we've been hiding behind for years.

Humans love the practice of labeling each other, because doing so gives us the illusion of control and safety-as though we've got a grasp on the totality of who the person is and what we can expect from them.

We might grow suspicious or uncomfortable when others surprise us, either by changing or revealing who they always were. But, research tells us that those sticky labels carry long-term consequences {11}. They absolutely create disharmony and division. In the majority of cases, we're destructively off-base-deluded by our own biases, fears and prejudices, almost certainly missing a universe of information. Worst of all, we're violating another person's right to evolve beyond the blueprint we created for them-one they probably never agreed to follow in the first place.

So, consider the labels you've been stamped with throughout your life, from the names you've been called to the ways people have bragged about you and claimed to know you. Perhaps you were the class clown or the popular girl that all the guys gawked at and talked about in the locker room. Or, maybe you were the outcast or the loser or the once-celebrated all-star whose reputation was ripped apart when you caused the team to lose the state championship.

Regardless of how you were labeled, here's the real deal: you're not defined by what you've lost or won, or the failed relationships that cracked your heart open, or the people who thought you were hot. And whether your mom or dad or aunt or grandmother labeled you "the smart one" or "the athletic one" and your brother or sister or cousin "the beautiful one," even with the best of intentions, their words were never the gospel. No human's words are the gospel.

For every person who's ever judged or labeled you harshly, they've got a closet full of things you could judge about them. Even if they've done a better job than you at keeping those things hidden. Even if they aren't ready to face the truth about themselves. Everyone has a vault of secrets and shame stories tucked away somewhere. And, truly, people can only identify that which is already awake in themselves. In other words, what disturbs them most about you is almost certainly a shadow part of themselves trying to pop up and say hello. So, let the negative connotations and limitations dissolve. Know that you're allowed to step out of the box you're in, no matter how long you've been cramped inside of it. You're free to kick and yawn and stretch out and dance beyond those borders.

Because those labels aren't yours and never have been. They're merely a projection of another person's belief system or narrative. Which means you're not who your high school legacy says you are or who your overanxious, micro-managing ex-boss said you were, even if those people might've been somewhat accurate in ways at the time. You're who you choose to be, today-from the beliefs you feed to the values you uphold to the actions you consistently take.

Stop hexing yourself with who you never were anyway.

RADICAL ACTION:
BE IRRITATED NO MORE

Because if you don't get what you want in the tiny ways, you can't expect to get what you want in the big, shiny ways.

There's the loose hinge on your closet door that you have to wrestle back into place. The loathsome tangle of electrical cords behind your desk. The unsightly gunk (might be toothpaste, might be God-knows-what-else) that's stuck to a far corner of your bathroom mirror. The 10,000 spam emails you swear you'll eventually clear from your inbox.

And let's not forget the box of cups and plates you've been meaning to drop off at your local donation box for months. They're still rattling in the back of your car, knocking into each other obnoxiously, making you groan every time you make a sharp turn.

You know those things that make you grit your teeth, whatever they are. In fact, you've probably got a blur of mental sticky notes about them, overlapping in your brain. You've sworn, again and again, that you'll fix them tomorrow, or next weekend, or after you throw the birthday party, or once you knock out the time-sucking work project. Except you never get around to it.

Days become weeks, which then spill over into months. Maybe even years. You're still griping about them, sometimes being overwhelmed by them, but you've got more important things pulling at your hair, filling up the pages of your planner, screaming at you from your lengthy to-do list.

What if you considered that those tiny annoyances are collectively congesting your brain, driving you crazy, taking up precious real estate? Perhaps they're overcrowding the spaces where fun-loving coffee meet-ups with new friends, enchanting moon baths with your pen and journal, and money-making strategies might be longing to gather and chant for your fulfillment and prosperity? Might you consider that those collective irritations are more poisonous to your life than you've realized?

There's some science that says they likely are. A study performed by a group of social psychologists found that women who perceived their home to be cluttered had elevated levels of cortisol throughout the day {12}. This is not only damaging to your mental health, but to your physical health as well. High levels of cortisol can lead to a flight of hormonal issues, and are linked to anxiety, depression and fatigue, unhealthy weight gain, among other bodily threats {13}.

So, as an act of taking kind, loving care of yourself, carve out an hour or two today to build a strategy for eliminating the clutter and noise, once and for all. Use the pages that follow (and create more, should you need them). Set a date and time to address each irritation, and make its remedy non-negotiable.

Do it to reclaim your freedom and call your sanity back home. Do it as a favor to your bank account and your dearest relationships. Do it for all of the versions of yourself that the future holds.

If you don't love and respect yourself enough to get what you want in the tiny ways- including the ones that creak at you annoyingly, or add piles and tabs of chaos to your desk, computer or phone-how can you expect to get what you want in the big, shiny ways?

Like, for example, the shark of a publicist for your new book, the dream vacation in Saint-Tropez, the raise you earned two years ago, the like-minded confidante who's equally as jazzed about yoga, crystals and tempeh, or the affectionate and trustworthy romantic partner that you've been praying to lure into your vortex?

If you want to radically improve your life, and break out of the patterns that've stolen your peace and caused you a world of grief for way too long, you've got no more time for unnecessarily irritating yourself, day after day. This life presents us with enough gut punches as it is, so don't make any part of your journey more painful than it has to be.

You deserve doors that close with ease, serving bowls nicely organized on a shelf that you don't have to wobble on your tippy toes to reach, weighty emails you can find with a simple search, apps you can access with a quick scroll and a tap, and mirrors so sparkling clean you can see that beautiful, beaming face of yours.

You deserve to have it all. This is where it begins.

BE IRRITATED NO MORE:

*THINGS I LOVE AND RESPECT MYSELF ENOUGH TO REMEDY,
ONCE AND FOR ALL.*

☐

☐

☐

☐

☐

☐

☐

☐

BE IRRITATED NO MORE:

(CONT.) THINGS I LOVE AND RESPECT MYSELF ENOUGH TO REMEDY, ONCE AND FOR ALL.

- ☐
- ☐
- ☐
- ☐
- ☐

- ☐

- ☐

PHASE ONE

MY MOST POWERFUL REVELATIONS
DURING THIS PHASE HAVE BEEN...

_____

_____

_____

_____

_____

_____

_____

_____

_____

_____

_____

_____

_____

PHASE ONE

RADICAL DAILY 4 CHECK-IN:

ANY FLASHES OF CLARITY? REFRESHING TRUTHS?
SURPRISING ACTS OF COURAGE?

"YOU KNOW WHY IT'S HARD TO BE HAPPY — IT'S BECAUSE WE REFUSE TO LET GO OF THE THINGS THAT MAKE US SAD."

- BRUCE LIPTON
THE BIOLOGY OF BELIEF

PHASE TWO

REIMAGINE:

to revisit your limitations through a lens
of power, and to then swim freely
through the scope of what's possible;

to be open to the radical
reinterpretation of your potential and
worthiness in a way that unlocks
forgiveness and freedom, and makes
you tingle with curiosity,
wonderment and glee.

RADICAL EXERCISE:
IMAGINE IT FORGIVEN

*"May you be free, may you be happy,
may you be healthy, may you live with ease..."*

Once upon a time, I believed that forgiveness meant pardoning a betrayal as though it never happened-as though to slather a glossy coat of denial over the ways I'd been achingly wronged. But that was never it. Forgiveness doesn't say, "You know what? You're right. I totally overreacted about that. We're good."

Nope, it doesn't say that at all. It doesn't wave a magic wand and make someone's cruel or nasty behavior shiny and clean, and it doesn't mean you'll have amnesia about what happened. It also doesn't mean you'll never again be visited by the phantoms of disgust or fury or sadness. You might be. And, if so, you'll remember what to do.

Forgiveness is where you fling open the iron gates of bitterness and revenge, and start trekking toward freedom. It's where you let the compassion and respect and protection you have for yourself triumph over any burning need for vengeance. It's medicinal for *your* mental and emotional agility {14}. Because a spirit of flaming retaliation ensnares you in places where joy and luck and prosperity would never hang out in a million years. So, in essence, forgiveness is far more than a departure from agony and rage. Forgiveness is a sweet surrender and a personal victory. Forgiveness is an act of self-love.

One of the most profound exercises I've ever come across is from Jonathan Fields' soulful masterpiece, *How to Live a Good Life* {15}, and it's a testament to the power of releasing yourself from the giant black hole of contempt. The first time I moved through it, I felt like I'd been dropped into a warm, bubbly spirit bath. So, for this chapter, I want you to try it.

To begin, Fields asks that you speak the following mantra over yourself: "May I be free, may I be happy, may I be healthy, may I live with ease." Repeat it until you feel yourself gaining some loving momentum behind it-until you're flooded with feelings of appreciation for your life and have compassion for every decision you've ever made, regardless of the outcomes.

Next, call to mind someone you care for deeply, saying, "May you be free, may you be happy, may you be healthy, may you live with ease." In this space, bathe in gratitude for this person. Splash around it in. Immerse yourself in your love and well-wishes for them.

Imagine them smiling, tossing their head back in untethered joy, moving through moments doing their favorite things. Soaring through their days. Achieving and excelling. Imagine them being kissed by the sunshine. Getting everything they've ever wanted.

After a moment in that space, steer the sentiment toward someone you feel ambivalent about. But, again, envision this person in your mind, allowing compassion and good fortune to flow toward them, rocketing straight from your heart to theirs. No holding back. Send all of the love you've got because you know there's an infinite supply of it.

Finally, call to mind someone you're struggling to forgive-perhaps someone you might even think you despise. Like, say, the lover who abandoned you mercilessly, the friend who betrayed you or conned you and took advantage of your generosity, or the ex-colleague who swindled clients from your private files. Let the burn of resistance rise up. Stand in its furnace, knowing you've got a warrior of love inside of you that is braver and stronger than it'll ever be.

Repeat the mantra over and over until you feel all of your bitterness burn away. Feel yourself wishing that person genuine happiness and peace of mind. And, remember: this exercise is not about excusing what they did; it's about releasing yourself from the prison of what they did. It's an act of love for yourself and for humanity as a whole. It's more transformative than you can possibly imagine. This exercise will free you and allow you to align with the energy of goodwill. Soon, you'll be soaring into more beautiful and prosperous days.

The first time I worked through it, I wasn't prepared for the shift I was to experience. I crawled into bed, turned off the lamp and pulled the covers over my shoulders. With my husband and dog sleeping nearby, I shut my eyes and repeated the words in my mind. Slowly, I felt a subtle shift within my body as I spoke the mantra over myself. My muscles softened. My temperature warmed. My frequency rose.

Next, I turned my attention toward thoughts of my dad. Within minutes, cool tears streamed down my face. I envisioned him behind his house on the Florida bay, ambling across his boat dock, his fishing rod in hand and pelicans soaring across a powdery blue sky above him. I imagined him moving through his days feeling immeasurably joyful and light and peaceful and worry-free. I saw him laughing with my mom and tossing a bone to their dog, Sadie. With this vision fixed in my mind, I smiled tearfully into the dark.

I then moved onto an acquaintance who conjured no particular emotions for me. Again, I felt myself getting lighter and warmer, rising higher in frequency. Again, smiling into the dark. Wishing them happiness and good fortune and the fulfillment of their wildest dreams.

Finally, I thought of a person who triggered me so much, it made me wince. This person had made rude and belittling remarks to me and others I cared about-a couple of times making cryptic, self-serving jabs that attempted to minimize my relationship with my daughter. We're talking about the daughter I'd fought like hell to have and the bond I'd wept and waited my entire life to experience. So, yeah, this was a tough one.

I'd tried so hard to keep things harmonious. And, truly, sometimes things were lovely and generous, and I'd start to wonder if all of the problems had been in my head. I'd find myself searching for and celebrating the best in them. But, without warning, they'd turn cold and sour and punishing when they failed to get their way, or gloat about themselves while making a nasty and jealous dig about someone else. Alas, my anger with them would be swiftly reignited, and I'd feel irked with myself for having been so naive, yet again.

At first, forgiving this person felt like wrestling a bear. As though my brain was shouting to my heart, "Oh, hell no, sweetie! We're not going out like this!" But, after a red-hot moment or two, compassion came gliding onto the scene, and I began to view this person in a softer light.

Just like I'd felt hurt and wronged by them, I'd been guilty of hurting and wronging others, too. Just like I had subconscious insecurities that got in the way of me showing up as my kindest, most likable self, so did they. Just like they weren't the picture of charm and grace, neither was I.

Soon, it was as though a band of angels surrounded my bed, beaming over me, whisking me straight toward freedom. But it had only been made possible by my willingness to reimagine all of the hurt and fury and resentment I'd been holding onto...as forgiven.

IMAGINE IT FORGIVEN

PEOPLE, DECISIONS AND EXPERIENCES
I LOVE AND RESPECT MYSELF ENOUGH TO FORGIVE...

IMAGINE IT FORGIVEN

(CONT.) PEOPLE, DECISIONS AND EXPERIENCES
I LOVE AND RESPECT MYSELF ENOUGH TO FORGIVE...

BEDTIME STORY:

WHEN LIFE KNOCKS YOU DOWN, COME BACK TO WHO YOU ARE

...because you're about to find out that you're just getting started.

I felt like I'd been kicked in the teeth. I stared down at my phone screen in disbelief, reading an icy email that announced a magazine story I'd spent two years devotedly championing was officially on its deathbed. An editor had shot it in its big, beautiful heart, reducing its existence to a paragraph of a lackluster goodbye. "I'm so sorry this happened," she wrote. "Here's your updated contract so that you can submit your kill fee."

Excuse me, what? I was 7 months pregnant at the time, and this news brought a level of emotional injury that I was too hormonal to handle. And I for sure hadn't seen it coming.

For so long, I'd felt possessed to see the project through. I stole late hours while on a romantic trip in the Rocky Mountains with my husband. I burrowed in coffee shop corners in order to cram in moments of work in between other meetings. I pored over countless studies on the subject matter, interviewed 43 people across multiple time zones and channelled every shred of excellence toward fulfilling my end of the agreement. I saw it as my one giant, beaming lighthouse of opportunity and I was going to paddle or swim or backstroke or whatever the hell I needed to do to make it across the river, damn it!

My editor assured me, over and over again, that my efforts were going to be worth my while. I trusted that they would, finding bursts of euphoria within my diligence. But one of my scariest fears had come true. And, there I was-choking on the news that my hard work had been tossed into the wastebasket. As though it meant nothing. Except, to me, it meant everything!

I'd entrusted professionals with my idea, and they'd pulled the wool over my eyes in the process of its annihilation. Or, so it seemed. I felt cheated, manipulated, undermined and undervalued. And I was seething with anger.

Those monsters! How could they?

You can almost certainly relate, at least in some vein. And, when you're in that space, it feels like you're the only one slithering across those lonely, dejected grounds. But the truth is that no one gets a pass from pain. Trauma is a natural part of the human experience.

One study determined that, on average, a woman will experience 15 kisses, two failed long-term relationships and at least one massive heartbreak-the kind that sends her sobbing into her hands and pillows and steering wheel for weeks or months-before she finds lasting love {16}. Another showed that the average American gets their heart broken about five times between childhood and middle age {17}.

Oh, and in matters of business and entrepreneurship? Don't even get me started. One study concluded that, for every entrepreneur who succeeds, they almost certainly must, on average, fail miserably and publicly about 3.8 times {18}. Which means 3.8 times that they'll have no choice but to sip on a bitter cocktail of embarrassment and grief. Also the pressure to explain to an onslaught of inquiring minds why the world failed to fall in love with their beloved idea.

So, if you find yourself in those shadowy corners-whether you've been made to feel disposable, shamed or violated in some way, know that you aren't alone. Whatever may've inspired you to purchase this program-whether a big, shining career opportunity vanished into the blackness, your precious relationship deteriorated without warning, or you've felt shattered and lost for way too long, now that you've determined all that needs to be purged, it's time to reimagine a future that's paved with resilience and possibility.

Let me breathe some truth back into your confusion, doubt or sorrow: you're not only capable of finding joy, love and purpose on the other side of misfortune, but you must. Ahead are five incontestable reasons to pick yourself up, dust off your knees and reclaim your power in the midst of whatever it might be.

The simple fact that you've made it this far into the program is confirmation that you've got what it takes to prosper on the other side of whatever it is. You're about to lock arms with a level of confidence and unstoppability you never dared to dance with before. You're about to start remembering who you are.

1 The failure, loss or setback, no matter how grave, doesn't define you.

Just as you're not defined by a single birthday, you're not defined by a single event. You're not characterized by another person's ability to validate your worth, align with your ideas or honor your time investment. You're the most important person you can ever lose, and if you're reading this, it means your lungs are still breathing in air and your heart is still pumping blood. You've still got you.

Melt into this knowing, allowing it to make you fiery and dangerous. Because when you're no longer willing to be puppeteered by a bad day or month, or by another person's nod of approval, you no longer have anyone rationing out your power.

2 You've got resilience in your DNA.

If you explored your lineage, examining the lives of your parents and grandparents, or perhaps shuffling back multiple generations to uncover a riveting tale of survival that rocks you, you'd find evidence of those who persisted through the unimaginable. Maybe they survived a war, or a famine, or a vile injustice, or a disastrous act of God. Maybe they birthed 12 chubby babies...without even so much as a Tylenol. Even if you've got no way of uncovering your family history, know this: There are conquerors and heroes and good-doers somewhere in your bloodline. Probably many of them.

The point is, don't let a lousy outcome or situation cause you to forget the power that's embedded within your legendary roots. Call upon the fighting spirit within you. Tap into the courage and vigor that you inherited, right there in your cells. This situation, albeit stressful or sad or perhaps horrific, isn't mightier than you. It truly isn't. Your heart might be broken, but your story isn't over. Not unless you decide that it is.

3 You're the boss of your self-belief.

Going back to the first chapter of this book, remember that you call the shots from here on out. Which is also to say that, if you've allowed some higher-up at your workplace, or a dangling carrot of a career opportunity, or some alluring love interest, or a mean girl in your social circle to act as the CEO of your self-belief, it's time you fire them. For good. And never again give another person authority over the way you perceive yourself. It's no one's responsibility to dash into your bad day, validate your hopes and handcuff you with confidence. That's a job only you can fulfill. And it's the most important one you'll ever have.

4 Every person you admire has fallen hard and fast on their face.

Remember that statistic I hit you with at the start of this chapter? Every celebrity or influencer you emulate, every entrepreneur you look to for inspiration, and every mega-successful company you roll out your hard-earned dollars to support has been slammed with a setback so severe, they were sure their glory days were over. They may've wallowed in the bloodbath of a plan that was once high-kicking with promise, but lost its pulse.

Vera Wang's story of personal reinvention is a compelling one. Long before she designed and sold millions of high-end wedding gowns, she was a figure skater who failed to make the cut for the U.S. Olympic team. And, in the years that followed, she graduated from college and ventured into the world of editorial, accepting employment at *Vogue* magazine. She gave the publication 17 years of her creative passion and literary expertise before being rejected for its editor-in-chief position.

I can imagine she was probably blindsided by the rejection. But, as defeated as she may've felt at the time, that slamming door rerouted her toward the endeavor she was most meant to fulfill-the one that launched a multi-million dollar fashion empire. In fact, according to *Forbes*, Wang's estimated net worth was $420 million in 2016 {19}. That's a hilariously superior figure to what she might've earned as *Vogue*'s editor-in-chief.

Within every shining success story, there exists a tale about a thing that was so furiously wanted once upon a time, but never had. While it's essential to give yourself plenty of open air and gentleness to grieve, don't make yourself at home there. Your most lucrative opportunity could be whistling right around the corner, chanting for your arrival.

5 Meet your new mantra: "Every rejection is rerouting me in a more powerful direction."

Sometimes the most commemorative chapters of our lives are only made possible by the disappointing ones that came before them. There's always a magic lesson behind every closed curtain, and a rebirth yawning and stretching in the midst of every ending. Even if it doesn't feel like it at the time.

After I recovered from the shock of editors murdering my story, I saw the opportunity within its death. The truth was that theirs wasn't the only quality media platform to champion the story to the public-not at all. I'd hinged everything on their willingness to publish it, but that slamming door gifted me with the ability to exercise my resourcefulness and discover what I'm made of. And, most deliciously, two months later, after another powerful media source had published a different slant on the issue, I got yet another email in my inbox-this time asking me to resuscitate it. This time, they were waiting on me. Which only served to give me negotiating edge.

Make no mistake about it-I was for sure poppin' my collar. It was a dynamite feeling to have finally proven that what I'd known all along-years before any other journalist or editor cared about the story-was urgent and true and worthy of being illuminated. But, ultimately, even if they'd never come crawling back to me, I got the chance to learn that there's freedom in every unraveling—even when unforeseen and definitely unwanted. Through the setback, tears and nauseating pit in my stomach, I was given a front-row seat to my own resilience. Instead of looking to them for my success, it forced me to turn within. I learned so powerfully much about myself through that experience.

So, congratulations, soul survivor. I'm applauding you for not turning your back on yourself, despite the crushing things that could've taken you out. And I'm buzzing with excitement because I know you're about to find out that you're just getting started.

Welcome to your Independence Day.

BEDTIME STORY:

IF OTHERS ARE LIVING OUT THEIR DREAMS, WHY NOT ME?

It's a whole lot easier once you realize it's a simple decision.

It was an unremarkable Labor Day weekend in 2007. Gina "Gigi" Butler, an Oklahoma native who'd transplanted to Nashville in pursuit of stardom, hovered over a toilet inside of an A-list country singer's home. She was surrounded by a tumble of sponges, mops and buckets. Polishing floors by day and crooning into a microphone by night, she'd devoted a full decade to her singer-songwriter aspirations. She believed she had talent, but nothing was happening.

Time had turned her dream from something that glistened with promise into something that felt cruelly elusive-like a carrot dangling barely out of reach. Thirty-two years old at the time, she'd garnered no interest from managers or label executives, and had no prospects humming in her orbit. She was realizing that her vision of chart-topping glory and roaring crowds had fallen on deaf ears. This was it. Her dream was flatlining.

Instead of walking the red carpets with the likes of Leann Rimes and Taylor Swift, she was pulling hair balls from their drains and emptying their trash cans. She was never going to be "Gigi the legend." She'd become "Gigi the cleaning lady for legends." Those were the breaks that life had sent her way, as the saying goes. Or, so she thought.

Mid-scrub, Butler's phone buzzed. The call was from her brother, who was zig-zagging through the streets of Manhattan at the time. She thought about not answering, but decided to accept the call and let him know she was too busy to talk. Nearly out of breath, she heard him say, "Hey, Gigi. I'm in New York...and I just spent two hours standing in a long line for a red velvet cupcake that's not as good as yours or mom's. Why don't you open up your own shop there in Nashville?"

It sounded ridiculous at first. *Was he kidding? A cupcake shop? C'mon.*

Except something about it landed strangely-almost like a wink from the divine. The more she sat with the crazy idea, a giant "What if?" began reverberating around her, increasing in volume, vibrating with possibility. Baking was in her blood. It had been passed down through generations of cellular memory. Besides, she wasn't afraid of hard work and she wasn't afraid to fail. What if this wasn't so insane, after all?

Butler ended the call, tucked her phone away and tried to shift her focus back to scrubbing, promising herself that she'd revisit the thought again later on. But her brother's words had become like an infectious melody looping in her head, without end.

A cupcake shop. Hmmmm…

She stood there, all alone, enveloped by decadence, covered in soapy pink latex from fingertips to elbow. Although grateful to have a steady income, this wasn't the life she'd envisioned for yourself. And it didn't look like her situation was going to change anytime soon, should she continue trekking along that path. Admitting this to herself, she turned away from the toilet and toward the mirror.

"I looked square into my own eyes, tossed my hands up in the air and said, out loud, 'Well?! Why not me?' I had already failed at my first dream, so I thought I may as well give another one a shot," Butler told me in an interview for a *The Connect* magazine feature story a few years ago {20}.

Two days later, she found herself drifting through the glass doorway of her local bank, trying not to stare at her hands, praying and hoping to convince the monetary powers that be to grant her a new business loan. Except it wouldn't go as smoothly as she'd hoped. "They all laughed in my face like I was a crazy person. A cupcake shop was a joke to them," Butler confessed in our interview.

Still, she felt possessed to see the venture through. Once she'd allowed the possibility to take root and had reimagined a more vivid future for yourself—one where she'd spend her days creating and sharing the sugary confections she'd always loved, there was no turning back.

"The feeling came from something beyond me. I told my family that God had shown me a glimpse of what was to come, and they thought I was out of my mind," she said during our interview.

After being hit with her fourth loan denial, Butler turned to cash advances on her credit cards, where she scraped together $100,000 to cover rent, ingredients and supplies so that she could open a small store in Nashville's sought-after Midtown neighborhood. In the dawn of a recession, and with a lowly $33 to her name, she did exactly that.

"Looking back, I think a lot of people felt sorry for me, almost like they thought it was a desperate move on my part. Some of my cleaning clients would say, 'Oh, honey, we'll buy a dozen from you." They were sincere in their support, but I think there was a lot of 'bless her heart' in it, too," Butler said.

Now, I want you to lean in closely and pay attention, because here comes the most scrumptious part of this story. This is the part that'll launch you from your seat. Not only did Butler's daring decision not crash and burn in the midst of a recession; it didn't become a one-hit-wonder, either.

On the afternoon of the shop opening, a line of customers were spilling into the parking lot. And they kept coming back... and back... and back again. Within a week, she had regulars-many of whom were gushing about their favorite flavors and sugary swirls to their families and friends.

And, in the years since Butler stowed her cleaning gloves away, she's stepped into an entirely different life. One that became an absolute explosion of success and notoriety. That phone call from her brother-the one she was almost too depressed to take-set in motion a monumental shift in her reality, spawning the world's largest, multi-million dollar cupcake franchise with 140 store locations, many of which are still boxing up delectable swirls of icing to this day.

She appeared on *Undercover Boss* {21} and wowed an audience with her tenacity and wisdom from the TedX stage. She authored her first book, *The Secret Ingredient: Recipes for Success in Business and Life*, and has been celebrated by entrepreneurial legends like Daymond John of *Shark Tank*, and featured in dozens of top media sources like *Forbes* and *Business Insider*.

A few months ago, I spotlighted Butler's amazing story for another lifestyle magazine. We chatted about the highs and lows of entrepreneurship, and she got candid about the hard stops and slow starts, mighty wins and dizzying losses she's danced with along the way, since she exploded onto the scene as a culinary contender. Because that's life. That's what happens when you take risks.

But her willingness to bet on herself is something she'll never regret. That decision continues to gift her with so exceedingly much. It opened up a wealth of probability. It spawned a domino effect of accomplishments, experiences and recognitions that no one can ever take from her. It's taken her places she never could've gone otherwise. Because of it, she's got an array of delicious accolades and memories.

Some might say that Butler got lucky-that talent and timing had spun together at random, blanketing her in favor. That, perhaps, the stars had aligned that day. And, maybe so. But not entirely.

Because none of it-absolutely none of it-would have been possible had she not had the guts to ask herself, "Well?! Why not me?"

REIMAGINE

I'm pretty sure if you're here, you survived
the awkward middle school years.

You know exactly what I mean.
The trauma of growing pains, gym class and acne.
Hideous haircuts. Learning how to move in a body that
feels completely foreign and is suddenly too big or long
in places it wasn't big or long two weeks ago.
First crushes found and lost.
Probably braces and a retainer, too.

That's a gobsmacking level of resilience,
when you think about it. Which is also to say that,
you've got resilience in your DNA. All you have to do is
call upon what you already know how to use.

Because, if you can endure a few disorienting years of
one self-conscious fiasco after the next, and live to tell
about it, you can overcome anything.

You're as unstoppable as you decide to be.

laceyjohnson.com

BEDTIME STORY:

BLESS THE TRAIN
THAT BROUGHT YOU HERE

...and rev your engine of epiphany and transformation while you're at it.

One morning, in between the usual eye rubs and yawns, I lay propped up against a stack of pillows, snuggled under my bed sheets, scrolling through my Instagram feed. Dressed in saucy red yoga pants, a grey crop top and white sneakers, there was *Lisa, a fiery, outspoken, 30-something mother of two whose selfies often showcased beads of sweat dripping from her hairline. Every inch of her sculpted flesh was a sight for swooning eyes.

I'd been casually following her fitness journey for the better part of a year. She documented her daily ritual of leg lifts, dancing arms and mountain climbers for her followers, oftentimes with her infant daughter napping peacefully in a plush bouncer nearby. Most days, candles flickered and incense danced in a loop of smoke behind her.

"I can't say enough about what the Tracy Anderson Method has done for my body," she often raved. "I haven't been this fit since high school."

Having boasted more than 40 pounds of postpartum weight loss, her will, determination and cheerful attitude were even more inspiring than her gorgeous selfies. She looked radiant, with a confidence in her gaze that was absent from her earlier posts. "Tracy's crazy ab exercises are even helping to close my abdominal gap," she'd once gushed.

But, on this day, her words nearly gave me whiplash. On this day, she was announcing that, after two years of sweaty devotion, she'd stepped off of Tracy Anderson's train and leapt onto another-one of her ex-muse's most vocally critical competitors, in fact. And it appeared that she was hustling for all of her travel companions to come along with her. It appeared she was one flame away from setting Tracy's train on fire.

I scrolled back a bit, and noticed another post from the week before where she'd made a bullet point list of why Tracy's was no longer the magical fitness method on high, but, quite suddenly, had become inadequate in comparison to her newest discovery. There were vague mentions of "having no muscle tone with TA," finding the repetitions to be boring, and a recent weight gain of five pounds.

Huh? It was so weird. And confusing.

I scrolled through the post comments and confirmed that her other followers had been equally as blindsided. And, while poring over Lisa's responses, it was almost as though she wasn't so much trying to convince others as she was hoping to convince herself-as though she believed that she had to burn down Tracy's train in order to fully commit to the new one she was on.

Never mind that the train she was so passionately derogating had brought her safely to her current destination-40 pounds lighter, tighter, more mentally disciplined and overall healthier. How it had jump-started her fitness lifestyle and infused her with a renewed sense of self-belief and direction. How it had been the precise vehicle that had driven her straight to this newfound fitness kingdom she was so suddenly infatuated with-one she'd only been gallivanting around for less than three weeks.

Sayonara, baby. Out with the Tracy Anderson Method and in with the new. It just didn't make sense. Or, maybe it did?

In my almost-decade of reporting and creating content in the realm of self-development and mental health, I've noticed something. So often we believe that we have to denounce the ghost of who we were or where we've been in order to embrace the vision of who we wish to become. But it's not true. We're not required to hate something in order to love something that's replaced it-not a new city, or a career move, or a life stance, or a fitness program. Or anything that's a part of who we're becoming, which includes all of the versions of ourselves that we've ever been.

For so long, I shivered at the thought of the little girl I once was: the blonde-haired, suddenly motherless 6 year-old who stared at her hands a lot because she was tired of being stared at with pitying eyes. The one who learned to zone out because she was tired of being whispered about in between the church pews. The one whose tights were often bunched in a corner of her patent leather shoes because she didn't know how to put them on as well as her mother had. The one who ached to take her big sister's tears away.

Also the one who often felt as though she was screaming at the top of her lungs, "Help! Help! I'm hurting, too! I need you to listen! I need you to ask how I'm doing and care about my answer! I know more than you think I do!" But she felt as though no one could hear her.

She represented angry outbursts and awkward pauses and long, stressful silences and an upset stomach. She was the one who clung to her father for dear life-mostly because he did things like show up for her first grade Mother's Day party at school, knowing that, otherwise, the chair beside her would've been empty. She had questions coming at her that she didn't want to answer. But also questions that no one ever bothered to ask. She had shame and pain and loneliness and uncertainty.

And she had a home that was filled with rows of dresses and high heels and hot rollers and coffee mugs-totems of a bubbly, gorgeous, mocha-haired mother who seemed to have vanished into thin air and was never, ever coming back. The one whose laughter would never again fill those walls. The one who'd "gone to Heaven." Whatever that meant.

Through the various subconscious reprogramming exercises and healing modalities that we've been working through together in this book, as well as other therapies such as hypnosis, EMDR, acupuncture and somatic bodywork, I learned how to reconceptualize the aversions, disempowering beliefs and sensitive emotions I held about that little girl, as well as the traumatized teenager and frazzled young adult that spawned from her.

If you want to live an empowered, expansive and love-filled life-one that feels full and safe-this is essential for you to do as well. I can't emphasize this enough.

A few months ago, I interviewed Terri Cole, licensed psychotherapist and author of *Boundary Boss*, for an *Oprah Daily* story, exploring the "why" and "how-to" of a self-discovery journey {22}. She's become one of my most trusted mental health sources as of late, mostly because she's got a knack for unpacking complex and heavy topics in a way that makes you feel naked, but also unconditionally accepted, honored and seen.

During our conversation, I asked her, "Would you say that self-discovery starts with self-recovery? Does it begin with combing through your subconscious, and gutting your early childhood indoctrinations, and assessing your wounds, and reimagining something different?"

Her answer was golden. She said, "Taking a childhood inventory is a key part of any self-discovery journey, though it's the part that most people want to avoid. But, oftentimes, you have to go back to the scene of the crime to understand why you are the way you are and why you're sensitive to certain things. Because only then can you truly, mindfully give yourself permission to choose something different or ask for what you need. The child inside of you needs to be acknowledged so that you can give the adult 'you' permission to stop over-functioning or running or whatever it is that's been keeping you from fully knowing yourself."

How breathtaking is that?

I've learned to embrace every embarrassing, stomach-turning, unsatisfactory angle of myself and my complex history. I love each of those girls and women, because they each had a hand in leading me here. I bless every train that carried me to the kingdom I'm currently living in-including the broken-down, fuming, shit-show ones. I'm proud of them and they're proud of me. They're my ghosts and my children and my sacred signposts and my teachers and my encyclopedias of empathy and wisdom.

And, so, I hope you're willing to embrace and love-and, perhaps, vindicate-each of yours.

You don't have to assault your previous endeavors, lifestyles, paradigms or stances in order to crown your new ones. You don't have to set any bridges on fire or burn any old love letters in order to get on board with who you're becoming, unless doing so would free or serve you.

You might cringe at the thought of some of your expired beliefs, habits, interests and outcomes, sure. Now that you know better, you might feel a few lifetimes away from the way you once felt and thought and showed up in the world. Still, you don't have to annihilate the person you were in order to build the one you're becoming.

Should a butterfly be repulsed by the caterpillar that it once was? Should it deny ever having been the caterpillar at all? I don't think so. Without the caterpillar having spun through its metamorphosis, the magnificent butterfly would never have emerged.

So, please, bless the train that brought you here. Even if it sucked. Rev your engine of epiphany and transformation. Let yourself shine in a way that would make the old train so proud of how far you've traveled. Blaze these roads with freedom of where you were and aren't anymore. All of those people live on inside of you.

You're all of them and they're each lucky to have been a part of you. And so much more...

RADICAL ACTION:

EAT FOR YOUR SOUL

...because your taste buds are a gateway leading straight to divinity.

The world is constantly flinging distractions your way. Commanding your attention from flashy billboards. Seducing you from fragrance ads. Inundating you with spam emails and push notifications about the latest launch, promotion or sale.

There's more information being hurled your way than ever before in human history-always tugging at your insecurities, rendering your mental capacities under siege, shouting, "This is the answer! Buy this! Wear that! Click here!" Which might explain why you sometimes forget how to pause and breathe and relish the moment.

You might count down the minutes of your workout until the final repetition. You might rush through a cup of coffee or a glass of wine so you can pour another. Perhaps you live for the weekends or for your next sun-drenched vacation. Always reaching for the next bite, the next chapter or the next milestone. But, in doing so, you're robbing yourself of the sweetness of living. Because your senses collectively serve as a gateway to your soul.

When I gave birth to my daughter almost two years ago, I felt like I'd been dropped into the grandest love story of a lifetime, but also into a whirlwind of sleep-deprivation and colic-induced disorientation that bordered on an identity crisis. As though I were Alice having found herself wandering deliriously adrift through Wonderland. In that space, I felt a gravitational pull toward my grandmother's house, where I could taste and smell the pancakes and strawberry cake I'd eaten as a child. My fragile, overstimulated psyche needed the safety and familiarity of seeing her barefoot in her kitchen, dressed in her bathrobe, stirring a pot of homemade fig preserves and pulling pans of hot biscuits from the oven.

So, when my baby was 3 months old, I did exactly that-packing up my breast pump and bassinet for a week at her house. And it proved to be medicinal. Rummaging through the same oak-stained snack drawers and snooping through the same refrigerator I once ransacked after school was a spa retreat for my spirit.

So, while most times call for foods that nourish your cells, today I want you to eat exclusively for your soul.

This is a powerful act of self-love because psychologists have long determined that we hold strong emotional attachments to certain foods from around the age of 7. Eating these foods-the ones we've created warm and wonderful experiences around, especially during our most formative years-can arouse deep, unconscious memories in a way that's intensely therapeutic {23}.

So, consider this your invitation to build a soothing and scrumptious spread of indulgence for the truest, most eternal part of you.

Like, for example, the bowls of buttery popcorn you passed around with your siblings as a child. The award-winning meringue your grandmother hauled to every holiday gathering. The charcuterie board of cheeses and jams and warm olives that your mom built on Saturday nights every October. Maybe the hot fudge and ice cream sundaes that you and your college roommate once wrecked your kitchen in an effort to make during finals week-a memory that has since burrowed itself into such a warm and tender place in your mind.

You've got nothing but freedom to interpret this activity however you wish. It need not be fancy or elaborate or sizzling with culinary pizazz, unless you want it to be. There's no one to impress here. No one but yourself.

Whatever your menu of choice, make sure it wraps you in a cocoon of rejuvenation and safety. Make sure it reminds you of why you deserve to be blanketed in comfort and pleasure and support.

Make sure it satiates the part of you that might be starving most.

BEDTIME STORY:

THE SLOW, STEADY SHUFFLE WINS THE RACE

It's not a fabulous feeling to be left in the dust, but what if it were only for a season or two-so long as you never strayed from your path?

The year was 1983. One-hundred and fifty young athletes gathered across the grounds of the Westfield Parramatta shopping centre in Sydney, Australia, buzzing with anticipation, refilling their water bottles and stretching their limbs in preparation for the 544-mile-long Melbourne Ultra-marathon. At the time, it was the longest and most intensive race of its kind.

A 61-year-old potato farmer by the name of Cliff Young arrived, dressed in overalls and work boots. Most of the other runners were well-trained athletes with svelte physiques and youthful vigor, around 30 years of age. They chuckled amongst themselves, amused at the sight of the old man in his farmer attire.

As Young approached the registration table and asked for his competitor number, observers were convinced that he must've been a part of some publicity stunt. Or, worse, gravely delusional. Onlookers gazed with intrigue and snickered with pity as he pinned his number, 64, onto his raggedy overalls.

They chatted amongst themselves: *Surely he's suffering from some kind of mental illness, right? Somebody, please stop him! What if he kills over?*

Reporters rounded up their camera crews, encircling him, each determined to be the first to hear his reasoning for being there. Though privy to their skepticism, he didn't seem bothered. When one of the reporters challenged his ability to cross the finish line, Young was undaunted, responding, "Yeah, I can. See, I grew up on a farm where we couldn't afford horses or four-wheel drives...whenever the storms would roll in, I'd have to go out and round up the sheep.... Sometimes I would have to run those sheep for two or three days. It took a long time, but I'd catch them. I believe I can run this race."

When the marathon kicked off, the entire pack of contestants blazed past him. The crowd laughed as he traipsed along the path with a leisurely shuffle. It was a perfectly hysterical sight. What was he thinking participating in an ultra-marathon, against professionally-trained athletes, no less? He'd had to remove his dentures because they rattled obnoxiously as he shuffled along, disrupting his momentum.

As the race progressed across the Land Down Under, Australians were glued to the live telecast, anxiously watching the old man, convinced he'd die before landing in the outskirts of Sydney {24}.

It was common knowledge that it'd take about seven days for the average runner to finish the race, and competitors had determined that the best strategy was to run for an 18-hour stretch, then rest for six.

Now, are you ready for the most hilariously brilliant part of this story? Young had no knowledge of this sleep standard. So, because he was so out of the loop, he had no plan to rest at all. In fact, as far as he knew, sleeping wasn't an option.

As the sun set on the first day, Young was trailing the pack by an extreme margin. But, when all of the sprightly, young, professionally-trained runners stopped to catch some sleep, Young shuffled on. And, by the end of the fourth day, Young, who'd been imagining that he was chasing sheep and trying to outrun a storm, surpassed them all.

Insane, right? Yeah, well, this story gets even better. Not only did he run the Melbourne to Sydney race at age 61, without sleeping or vomiting or killing over, and not only did he breeze past all of his younger, more 'qualified' doubters but, on the fourth day, he won first prize. That's right. He shut all of those dismissive, swaggering blabbermouths right up. And it wasn't a close race, to put it delicately. Young won by 10 hours, beating the record for that distance by a whopping nine hours. And he didn't stop at that. In 2000, an elderly man in his 80s, Young was back at it again, achieving a world age record in a six-day-long race in Victoria.

I love this story so much, for a multitude of reasons. But, what hits me the most is his graceful, unexpected comeback.

In life, it's not a fabulous feeling when everyone seems to be blazing past you, effortlessly. Your peers might be charging forward in their success with their heads held high-perhaps scoffing at your ineptitude. You might come to feel so dishearteningly left out as you watch others close on their dream homes, fall in love, build families, crush their fitness goals or gain lofty promotions. But, what if that feeling were only for a season or two, so long as you stayed alert and diligent on your own path? So long as you started believing-*really* believing-in what you bring to the game?

Because, much of the time, it's not about who's in the lead when the first gunshot fires, but about how determinedly you press on when it gets exhausting and hard. Because, sometimes, the most slow, steady and stubborn of all takes home the prize.

BEDTIME STORY:

THE RIFLE IN THE GROUND

You've got one fragile, gorgeous life that could expire at any moment.
If you knew it were the end, what would you wish you'd have said or done?

"We regret to inform you that your son was seriously wounded in action in France eight December."

I traced my fingers along the words printed on the 72 year-old Western Union telegram. It had yellowed over time, and was contained under a sheet of plastic in a well-preserved black binder.

The document was dated 1944, a time when roughly 70 million tender souls had been summoned to serve in the armed forces of the Allied and Axis Nations {25}. Some would kiss their mothers goodbye, never to stand on native soil again.

Others would return years into the future, eager to fill the pages of journals and scrapbooks, and to enlighten the ears of their siblings and offspring for generations to come. Perhaps, for many, it was the only way to purge the ugliness they'd seen-to get it out of them somehow.

As we continue moving through the process of reimagining your life story, I want you to let your heart lead you through this chapter. Here, I'm going to share one of those stories with you, as told to me a few years ago by a World War II Veteran-95 years old at the time. His blue eyes spilled with tears as he spoke of an age too chilling to forget.

**

In a blacked-out jeep, swirling across the muddy roads on the outskirts of France, American soldier James Howell Peebles, age 23, was transported into action on Halloween night, as an auxiliary fire lit up the darkness surrounding him. One minute he was shoulder-to-shoulder with his fellow combats, and the next he was darting across a muddy field and cowering into a foxhole that had been dug by the hands of a stranger who'd already come and gone. Perhaps a stranger that was still alive, but perhaps not.

As the guns fired, the ground quaked beneath his feet. He had officially entered the war.

Soon, the sight of German fighter planes crashed and scattered among the grounds he walked upon would become commonplace. And, he would learn that no man's psyche, regardless of how well-armored, was safe from war's dark and devouring perplexities.

One day, a sergeant, revered by the young soldiers for his cheerfulness and courage, bolted across the swampy terrain, howling inconsolably, "I can't do this! I can't take it. I'm going to get out of this!" The reality of death loomed over the men like a phantom, and, this time, it had swept in and conquered one of them. Almost like a mighty, towering tree branch snapping in a vicious storm.

One afternoon, Peebles wandered out of the muddy line to fill his canteen, moving to the edge of the field where the water was so clear, he saw the grass swaying beneath it. It was a glimpse of serenity amongst the unimaginable chaos. After quenching his thirst, he lifted his gaze, spotting a row of German bodies dangling above him in bloody defeat. He then realized that the water he'd been drinking had sifted straight through their decaying flesh. Peebles told me that this was his "most vivid picture of death."

Except for when it brushed up against him.

It was December 7, 1944, a snowy Thursday morning on the French battlegrounds. In the midst of battle, Peebles was struck by an explosion of mortar fragments, piercing his right thigh and left side of his chest. The pain jolted him. His body collapsed to the earth with a hard clunk.

Minutes later, a medic rushed to his side, tossing sulfur powder onto his wounds, pulling his ammunition bag up under his head, folding his raincoat over his torso, and, finally, inserting his rifle upright into the ground. This signified only one thing: young Peebles would soon be bowing out.

The chill in the air was unmercifully biting, and many times he dipped below the threshold of consciousness before resurfacing to the cold and the pain and the pandemonium yet again. Each time he was greeted by the rocketing of gunfire. He'd continue to lie there all day, with no morphine to mute the pain. His rifle stood upright in the muddy earth alongside him, serving as both his companion and an announcement to all that his minutes were a dwindling number.

At the tender age of 23, he'd reached his final minutes of life.

Shortly after 4 p.m., once darkness had swallowed the day, he heard a shuffle of feet approaching from the distance. Peebles called out to the noise, announcing, "I'm alive! I'm alive!" His rescuers' whispers sliced through the night air. "Ssshhh!" they exclaimed. "We don't know if the Germans are out here!"

The men then loaded his mangled body onto the litter and hauled him to the road, trampling upon shells and craters, where the Jeep would transport him to a nearby American field hospital. He'd have surgery and recover slowly over the coming weeks. Miraculously, Peebles had survived the blast. He'd live to tell.

But he knew what his final minutes on Earth felt like. And he'd never not know it. Decades later, a great-grandfather at 95, his voice shook as he relived the memory. Because, once you feel the breath of death in your midst, you're never the same person again.

***

Almost a year ago from the time of this writing, several years after my afternoon spent with Peebles, I, too, met my rifle in the ground. While pushing my 18-month-old daughter in her stroller across a bustling mall parking lot, I felt a monstrous weight from behind slam into my hips, shove me to the ground and crush my left shoulder, arm and hand–the tire slamming to a stop less than two inches from my skull.

For seconds that stretched on for 1,000 lifetimes, I knew I was about to die. This was it. When they say your life flashes before you in your mind's eye, and that everything is relived all at once, it's true.

There'd be no more gnawing on my daughter's button chin or burying my face into her buttery neck that smelled like maple syrup and pancakes. No more slow-dancing to Etta James and Sam Cooke in the kitchen with my husband as our dachshund, Lucy, scurried at our feet. No more rambling video chats with my best friends. No more delighting over the first spring bloom or sipping chilled lemonade on rooftop patios in the summer. No more flushed cheeks and fuzzy sweaters in October, or pulling the tree from the attic at Christmastime. No more chances to say and do and write all of the things I'd failed to say and do and write. No more chances to repair all the ways I hadn't kept my word to myself.

Goodbye, world. Lacey was bowing out.

A few hours later, an emergency room doctor gasped at the sight of my ripped, bloody flesh, taking inventory of the tire marks stamped across the shoulder of my shirt and all over my jeans. He looked at me as if I were a ghost, disbelieving that I'd survived being full-body run over and swallowed by a car's undercarriage.

And, miraculously, my daughter, though shaken by the experience, had suffered only superficial scratches to her head. She'd been buckled in tightly to her stroller, and I'd tossed her away to safety in the midst of the impact. Though I was teeming with trauma for days and weeks after–wandering into her bedroom at all hours of the night, just to touch her and smell her, I knew we'd experienced a loving brush with the supernatural.

And, listen, when death winks at you, you'll never live the same way again. You can't dance with its finality without changing forever. I know what my last second on Earth feels like, and I'll never not know it.

So, allow me to remind you of how fragile you are. This is no dress rehearsal, as they say. This is it. Today might even be your final curtain call.

With this in mind, my question to you is this: What would your rifle in the ground say about how you spend your days? The causes you contribute to? The ways you search for the humanity in others? Your willingness to admit when you're at fault? Your willingness to stand firm in what you believe.

You've got one fragile, gorgeous life. One that could expire at any moment. I want you to yank your rifle from the dirt and wave it high while you still can.

And, finally, I want you to ask yourself:

Am I who I want to be? Not the "me" my mom or dad or spouse says I should be. Not the "me" my cultural indoctrinations say I should be. Not who the Instagram influencer with the shiny, filtered hair and impossible thigh gap says I should be. But the "me" I long to be. The one I know is in there, dying to live and stand tall and speak out. Am I living as that person?

So, are you? Are you in there? Are you willing to crawl from hiding and live your days with a fullness of attention and curiosity and vivid, authentic expression, for however many you've got left?

Goodnight, beautiful soldier. When you're ready, let's reconnect for the next phase of this journey.

PHASE TWO

MY MOST POWERFUL REVELATIONS DURING THIS PHASE HAVE BEEN...

PHASE TWO

RADICAL DAILY 4 CHECK-IN:

ANY BOLD DECISIONS? NEW BEGINNINGS?
HEART-EXPLODING INSPIRATIONS?

"TO EXPERIENCE PEACE DOES NOT MEAN THAT YOUR LIFE IS ALWAYS BLISSFUL. IT MEANS THAT YOU ARE CAPABLE OF TAPPING INTO A BLISSFUL STATE OF MIND AMIDST THE NORMAL CHAOS OF A HECTIC LIFE."

- JILL BOLTE TAYLOR
MY STROKE OF INSIGHT:
A BRAIN SCIENTIST'S PERSONAL JOURNEY

PHASE THREE

LET THE LIGHT
& WONDER IN:

to be ignited with fires of hope and joy,
and to watch your curiosities, desires
and inspirations spring to life;

to draw back the shades of past
disappointments, limitations and regrets,
and to then create a sparkling venue for
enchantment, joy and miracles
to come flooding in.

RADICAL EXERCISE:

FANTASIZE YOUR REALITY

It's reality's playful prerequisite, after all...

When I was a child, my idea of a good time was dreaming up other worlds, oftentimes in solidarity. Who needed a sandbox or a swing set when I could spend one starry-eyed hour after the next ambling about a mythical realm of my own creation (well, my bedroom)? My dad would tap on the door every so often, asking, "Lace? Is everything okay in there?"

It always was. Sometimes I was standing in the sunlit glow of a Victorian garden, balmy and flourishing with fragrant bloom. Sometimes I was aboard a pirate ship with a rowdy crew, swapping slang and shanties. And, sometimes, I was styled in a draping satin gown, leaning cooly against a chair of an Old Hollywood movie set, the air thick with the smoke of cigars, and serenaded by the smack of a clapperboard.

Fantasizing was my dearest past time, mostly because I genuinely enjoyed hanging out inside of my own brain. To me, there was a labyrinth of wonder in there. I think lots of children feel this way. But then adolescence happens. And then adulthood. And so on.

Once we depart the gates of childhood and cross over into the awkward realm of growing pains and peer pressure and body-consciousness, we gradually begin to shed our spirit of dreaming. And, then, through the monotony of bills and professional responsibilities, society shoves a muzzle over the hum of our imagination. We might stop delighting in our daydreams altogether, perhaps dismissing them as gluttonous or silly.

Of course, this comes after years of being force-fed reality checks and doom-filled warnings like...

"There's a lot of competition out there..."

"Seriously? Get your head out of the clouds."

"C'mon, be a little more realistic."

"Well, I'm glad you're excited, but I'd hate to see you get your hopes up."

We might decide that our fantasies are delusional. We're told they're a waste of time. But, are they? I don't think so. In fact, I'd like to serve up a fiery rebuttal to that perspective. Because the truth is, fantasy is reality's playful prerequisite. If reality is the harvest, then fantasy, when met with action, is the seed that made the harvest possible. Everything ever created since the dawn of time was once an idea at play.

Like, say, the flickering, nutmeg-scented candle to my left. The knitted magenta blanket strewn across my lap. The stack of folders bringing sanity to my editorial madness. The coffee mug with a hand-painted dachshund that I grabbed on a whim a few days ago. The cozy jazz playlist pouring out of my Sonos speaker. The documentary I watched last week that I can't stop thinking about. The technology that's making it possible for your human experience to collide with mine.

Also you. Yes, you read that correctly. Before you were a cluster of cells, or a cooing infant, or a smarty-pants teenager, or a stressed-out adult trying to renovate your life, you were a divine idea. Before your eyes ever shimmered in the sunlight, you were a flash of creative insight. Long before you and I were living, breathing stories-learning languages and splashing around in the ocean and falling in love and swaying to our favorite songs, we were a thought in our creator's mind. We're all direct consequences of imagination. And we're meant to continue the trend.

Dr. Martin Luther King, Jr. held a dream of equality and racial justice. And, though his life was cruelly ripped from him at 39 years old, his peaceful approach to civil disobedience continues to bless the world. Although we've still got a terribly long way to go as a society and certainly haven't realized the fullness of his vision, Dr. King's courageous heart improved the world for his children, grandchildren and future generations.

His dream directly set in motion urgent conversations about the vile nature of racial discrimination and oppression, impacting education, government, entertainment and so much more {26}. He didn't kick back and get lost inside of his fantasies of equality for all; he gave a pulse to those fantasies. He was a dreamer who dared to be a doer.

There's also Wilbur Wright and his younger brother, Orville, who had fantasies of taking flight, despite being told they were delusional. Despite all of their neighbors gossiping about their mother, writing off her sons as being nothing more than unruly, troubled boys. But aren't you glad they didn't let those doubters kill their dream? Or, say, Nirvana. Years before "Smells Like Teen Spirit" became an anthem for 90s teenage angst, Nirvana was an unknown Seattle-based band inspired by the Pixies. And, before *Back to the Future* scored more than $388 million in the box office {27}, becoming one of the most enduring films of all time, nearly defining a decade, Bob Gale and Robert Zemeckis were dreaming up a quirky, spirited teenager they called Marty McFly.

Yeah, and I've got one more. Before billions of children were captivated by *Harry Potter*, J.K. Rowling was an unknown writer on a crowded train en route to London from Manchester, frantically searching for a pen {28}. And, if she hadn't rushed to her apartment, and vomited every bizarre and enchanted fragment of the narrative onto the first page, she'd never have gone on to sell more than 400 million books.

Can you imagine if J.K. Rowling, somewhere in between childhood and adulthood, had come to believe her ideas were unworthy of pursuit? What if she'd dismissed them as being lame or ridiculous? Which is also to say that, what if *Harry Potter*'s legendary wizardry had been stashed in the bottom of her desk drawer, under a pile of old holiday greeting cards and pharmacy receipts, tossed into the graveyard of abandoned dreams?

What a shame that would've been, you know?

As we stand at the halfway point of this program, I want you to begin to entertain the fantasies swirling about your brain. Even the ones that seem impossible or juvenile. Perhaps there's inspiration for a rapturous screenplay or an intricate line of snow globes, or maybe there's an app idea or a movement that would make millions of lives a whole lot easier or safer.

Whatever colorful and magical things are bumping up against each other in your mind, vying for your attention, drop them onto the page that follows, no matter how far-fetched.

Because one day, your silly idea might go on to captivate the hearts of millions of children, or forever alter the way the world communicates. Give readiness to the fantasies that make your body buzz with excitement. Acknowledge your most fantastical "what if"s with glee.

The future of humankind is counting on you, after all.

FANTASIZE YOUR REALITY

IDEAS, INVENTIONS & THEORIES I'VE GOT ZINGING ABOUT MY BRAIN:

BEDTIME STORY:

WHAT IF YOUR WEIRDNESS IS ALSO YOUR FIERCENESS?

Much of the time, those who've been blown off for not being "cool" or mainstream, are the ones who go on to make riveting history.

Humans are a fascinating species. We've got a slew of apps that track the latest innovations and trends in everything from beauty and fashion to real estate. We pore over Pinterest and YouTube for tricks that'll help us stand out from our competition. We're always observing and studying what everyone else is or isn't doing.

We want to make a statement so visually commanding and fabulous and enviable, others pause their scrolling fest to give us a tap of fleeting love. Many of us spend outrageous dollars on everything from handbags to hair appointments. We hide behind a pile of illusions and secrets. Society tells us to be that rare and special butterfly, so long as we don't stray too startlingly far from the norm or the expected. Because when we step into the party, we aim to make an entrance, sure, but not so much that anyone would dare point us toward the exit door.

We might smile when happy and poised are the stark opposite of how we feel, or nod and laugh when it's expected of us, even though we might not find the joke funny at all. We might hustle tirelessly to serve up our sexiest angles for our audiences-lifting our chins toward the most flattering light, inundating our phones with dozens of versions of the same constructed moment. Yet, how often do we shine a spotlight over the organically beautiful and interesting parts of ourselves-the stained and unpolished and worn-in parts that make us who we uniquely and vulnerably are?

Before I go on, please know I'm not discouraging you from being the most sexy or stylish or aesthetically smashing expression of yourself. Your body is a lovely piece of architecture and a creative outlet that you have the luxury of experimenting with until you've reached your tombstone. No one gets to dictate how any of those expressions or acts of self-care should look or play out. But, here's the rub: all of the world has become a stage, and we're sometimes suffocating underneath the characters we've created.

While we work to gain followers and hustle for applause, I think we should be equally as thoughtful about illuminating the raw and unedited truth of who we are. Because that's the only part others will authentically connect with. If you never reveal who that person is, you'll die never having been truly known...or loved. And how tragic would that be?

At the 2015 Grammy Awards, Sam Smith unpacked a potent message in his acceptance speech {29}, saying, "It was only until I started to be myself that the music started to flow and people started to listen... So thank you guys for accepting me for being just me."

Researchers in neuroscience have long determined that, as a species, we're biologically hardwired to be in community {30}. It's nearly as vital as food and shelter. In fact, studies show that people who live in prolonged isolation have shortened lifespans; the effect is comparable to smoking 15 cigarettes a day {31}. Which might explain why none of us are immune to the fear of being shunned by our peers. Being accepted is a primal instinct.

Still, the concept of authenticity is confounding to me because, as a society, we're so eager to applaud others for having been brave and radically transparent, all the while seldom relinquishing our fight against our own flaws. Which brings me to a pertinent question. What if the more lopsided and unfiltered angles of your personality and history-the ones that cause you to shiver with embarrassment or retract with shyness-are the ones that, if illuminated, would make you a magnet for connection, prosperity and fulfillment?

What if your inner oddball is actually your inner champion? What if it's your boss mode?

If everyone mirrored everyone else forever, how would records be broken or revolutions be inspired? If avant-garde or unconventional were never given the limelight, the world would never have known slapstick or stand-up. There'd be no Dave Chappelle. No *South Park*. No Chubby Checker inspiring an entire generation to do "The Twist." No Lizzo to empower your feminine wiles. No Jim Carrey or Quentin Tarantino. No Carol Burnett. No Prince, Kendrick Lamar or Billie Eilish. Or peanut butter and jelly. Or Nutella. Or Farrah Fawcett-inspired curtain bangs. I could seriously go on forever.

Let it be known that I know the lonely corners of the weirdo plight well. I've always felt a bit offbeat and strange and awkwardly Lucille Ball-ish. I talk passionately with my hands and eyebrows. I'm dramatic AF. My words flash across my face before my brain has the opportunity to edit them.

My laugh is loud and percussive and often employs my entire body-so much so that people have asked me dozens of times, "Um. Is that...real?" Also, when I'm zapped with a perceived injustice or an invasion of privacy, I nearly see flames. I can be a lot. A whole, fiery lot.

And, while I've never really been scant of friends who appreciate my quirks and passionate personality, there are some people who experience my energy as being too intense. What some people have described as "soulful," "entertaining" or "one-of-a-kind," others have described as "too much," "fake" or "annoying."

And, you know what? If so, that's absolutely their right. Not everyone's for me and I'm not for everyone. But I've come to embrace my enthusiasm as my divinity. Even when I'm so lost in the moment that I fail to tame my knee-jerk reactions, or I shuffle through my thoughts in haste and say an alarmingly moronic thing.

The word "enthusiasm" was derived from the Greek word "entheos," meaning "of God." Which means that, when I'm expressing myself enthusiastically, I'm giving the supernatural energy within me bigger wings. And that's going to get a little weird sometimes, at least by society's narrow standards.

So, here's the fantastically unpopular truth: if we spend our lives mimicking and modeling ourselves after others, throwing heavy covers over our idiosyncrasies and imperfections, we cheat ourselves and the world out of the gift of experiencing us. What this world craves-and desperately needs-is more people brave enough to be who they uniquely are, and fewer people influencing others about who they should pretend to be.

Influence culture is a trap; we need leaders who are willing to go their own way and make bold and conscious impact. We need people who aren't willing to hide from who they are.

Because, oftentimes, those who've been blown off or overlooked for not being attractive or talented or cooperative or mainstream enough are the ones who go on to unlock beautiful and revolutionary things in the hearts of others. Those are the people who make riveting history-the kind worthy of standing ovations. The kind that reveals and restores. The kind entire generations tear with joy to retell.

I'm so grateful for all of the oddballs and renegades who've been brave enough to not let their divinity be shoved into hiding. They embolden me to keep being me, whatever the cost. I think their weirdness is their fierceness. Maybe yours is, too.

BEDTIME STORY:

IMITATION IS A SLAP IN THE FACE TO YOUR GENIUS

...so stop screwing the world over and let your authentic brilliance step up to the mic.

In the days of Ancient Greece, it was believed that no human was more gifted than the next. If a person was especially brilliant, it simply meant that they were an open and willing receptor of divine direction. Every creative work was the result of a synergy between the supernatural and the natural worlds. It's how poems were written, how brush strokes moved across canvases and how mathematical concepts were downloaded and delivered to the masses.

During this era, the city of Athens spawned a battery of profound thinkers, including Socrates, known as the Father of Western Philosophy, his student, Plato, who explored innovative perspectives on justice and equality, and his student, Aristotle, who made massive contributions to metaphysics and mathematics. There was also Homer, one of the most revered poets of all time.

Athens wasn't a metropolis of decadence per se, but of fascination with the human experience. Its streets were overcrowded and swathed in filth—public bathhouses surrounding its bustling marketplace. The wine poured out as philosophical ideas were exchanged and theatrics were performed. Athenians were adventurous spirits and lavish dreamers with an expansive culture of thinking—not only producing the Parthenon and birthing the concept of democracy, but building ships and traveling far to Egypt and Mesopotamia to gather inspirations for architecture, language, medicine and more.

They were a curious society, too-always welcoming the bizarre and unknown. Why, though, was this city such a magnet for innovation? Perhaps, one might theorize, it was their allegiance to enchantment, and a willingness to get out of their own self-conscious way.

Socrates taught that inspired ideas could only land in human consciousness when a person was "beside himself," and "bereft of his senses." He spoke of having a divine attendant spirit, a "daemon," who he swore had been hanging out with him since childhood. These magical entities were believed to assist humans in ushering fresh concepts and inventions into the natural world. Socrates obeyed the commands of his daemon blindly and fervently. His philosophical contributions were only ever about tapping into an invisible realm and allowing himself to be an instrument for birthing them.

The Ancient Romans had a similar idea to the Greeks. They believed that every human had an actual "genius" who was assigned to him or her, beginning at birth. In other words, as far as they were concerned, there have never been any artistic or musical prodigies in human existence, but, rather, attentive and patient collaborators.

If the Ancient Greeks and Romans could speak to our modern society, they would likely say that when Freddie Mercury wrote "Bohemian Rhapsody," he had an inspired being looming over his piano, feeding him the chords and melody. The same could be said for Michael Jackson, who penned somewhere in the realm of 200 songs in his lifetime, earning 13 Grammys, and was famously quoted as saying, "You don't write the song, the song writes itself." Or, maybe, when fashion icon Karl Lagerfeld was burrowed inside of his Paris studio, curled over his sketchpad, he was in a séance with his genius, being guided through his next design.

This mystical approach to creative expression thrived until the Renaissance period, when human intelligence was suddenly tossed into the spotlight to take the credit for it all. This flung open the gates for all successful creators to run with their torches held high, basking in all of the applause and glory, but also carrying the burden in the event that their work crashed and burned. With this, brought the notion of scarcity, and most likely, bred the culture of artistic hierarchy, perfectionism and-you guessed it-the allure of imitation.

Today, our social media-driven world is oozing with more opportunities than ever to rip off the likeness of others. We can screenshot memes and quotes, copy blog posts and articles, and snag the styles we wish to emulate. Selfies are oftentimes captioned with words that weren't originated by the mind of the poster, yet made to seem as though they were.

Why do we do this? Is it a culture of entitlement? Laziness? Greed? Or, more specifically, might it originate from the fear that there isn't enough genius to pass around? That the universe isn't abundant with advancements, inventions and untold interpretations, but exists in a state of artistic famine? And, if so, what if we revisited the ancient concepts of what genius might mean?

What if we took a magnifying glass to some of the most influential artists and masterminds of our modern day, and found evidence that contrived imitation is not only reductive, but a slap in the face to the undiscovered ideas that might be tugging at our sleeves and wooing us-longing to be filtered through our individual expressions?

I believe that when you intentionally rip off somebody else, you're sort of blasting out an email into the universe that says, "Hey, everybody! Just confirming that I'm unworthy of your collaboration. Don't worry about hanging out in my art studio or moving through my pen; I'm just going to keep an eye on what Claudia and Hilary are doing over here."

When you intentionally suck somebody else's flavor, you're turning your nose up at the divine that wants to move uniquely through *your* eyes and hands and lips and feet.

Before I go further, I do wish to be clear about something, though. Imitation isn't the villain. It actually *does* have a useful place in society, so long as it's not allowed to link arms with the ego. A key mechanism in early cognitive development, children learn vital safety and social skills by watching and mimicking their parents and caregivers. This includes skills like how to properly pick up a fork and spoon, how to open a door and the manner in which they greet a cashier at a department store.

It also plays a role in developing empathy. A child's ability to imitate another person's actions allows them to "try on" other emotions and perspectives, and helps them grasp what it's like to be in another person's shoes. For example, have you ever been watching someone do or experience something-like, say, when a friend takes a nasty fall on the pavement and bloodies their knee, or an actor in a film is kicked in the stomach—and you can literally feel exactly what they must be feeling? You might grab at your own flesh and yell out, "Ouch! That was brutal. I felt that."

If so, those are neurons-often called "mirror neurons"-firing in the frontal lobe of your brain (the organ's "control panel")-performing a virtual reality stimulation of your mind {32}. And they're crucial because, if you want to really, truly empathize with someone's pain, you kind of need to "experience" it yourself. So, obviously, imitation isn't bad. It's actually important! But, when you camp out there, well into adulthood and use it as a means to pursue social acceptance, connection, security and success, you're screwing yourself-and the rest of the world-over.

I've got a juicy example of imitation gone frustratingly wrong, plucked from pop culture history. Long before Jessica Simpson built a billion-dollar fashion empire, she was a young star competing for the spotlight against Britney Spears and Christina Aguilera—oftentimes standing in their shadows. While they were dominating the covers of magazines and MTV's *TRL*, and sweeping awards shows, she, her management team and her label executives were probably strategizing for how to convince the world that she deserved to be ranked amongst the more famous blonde popettes.

Although Simpson's debut album *Sweet Kisses*, generated a *Billboard* Top 10 hit with the 1999 single "I Wanna Love You Forever," her appeal was only recognized in modest bursts. Her presence would start to soar, only to quickly fall flat. With her label executives hoping to elevate her star status, they orchestrated a more sensual image for her second album, *Irresistible*. For the title track and first single, the opening line revealed Simpson cooing in a breathy voice, evocative of a sex hotline advertisement. The accompanying music pulled back the curtain for Simpson's first appearance as the doe-eyed temptress.

They tucked her spray-tanned flesh into some sexy outfits, highlighting her cleavage and exposing her midriff, while she gyrated her hips, and exhibited forcibly pouty and seductive expressions and come-hither hand gestures. Although the single reached modest success, the majority of pop music enthusiasts weren't buying it. Most deemed her a "Britney wannabe." Her image came off as contrived and unnatural—a chintzy knock-off of the original thing.

In a 2003 interview with *Rolling Stone* {33}, while Simpson's career was in the midst of a massive revival, launched by the explosive popularity of her reality show, *Newlyweds: Nick & Jessica*, she reflected on that period, saying, "...I felt like I had to do what they did, like, I had to show my stomach and dance. But that's not me." Later that year, after her third album, *In This Skin*, spawned the mega-hit "With You," Simpson became a household name. It was the first time she'd co-written any of her own music, and it was the first time her real personality had ever been given a mic. In other words, if you were to ask the ancient Greeks or Romans for their take, they'd probably have said it was the first time she'd allowed the divine to move through her—the *real* her, not who she thought she wanted to be.

Nick Lachey, Simpson's husband at the time, spoke candidly about the sudden explosiveness of his wife's appeal, saying her career kept taking landslides in previous years because she'd never publicly stepped into the truth of who she was—the adorably big-hearted, bratty, sheltered, fashion-obsessed, Texas-born girl who was brilliant at serving up endless bloopers and cuteness.

The girl who didn't know that buffalo chicken wings were, in fact, not buffalo meat, and who was confused as to why cans of Chicken of the Sea tuna weren't packed full of chicken. The one who drove her husband crazy with her reckless spending habits. Who tossed dirty clothes and wet towels onto the floor. Who belched loudly and whined about folding the laundry. Also who wasn't made for performing oversexed, choreographed dance routines, but who wanted to sit on a stool and belt love songs from her heart.

America became full-on infatuated with Simpson—not despite her air-headed nonsense and brow-raising quirks, but because of them. Imitation intended to launch her but, instead, kept her from getting off the ground. It wasn't until she gave herself permission to stop imitating her competition—allowing the divine to work its magic authentically through her "girl's girl" personality and experiences—that she forged a real career and came into her own. Since that juncture, she's built the billion-dollar fashion empire.

In terms of widespread public success, she's a certifiable genius. Or, at least, she has one that she devoutly obeys. Either way, know this: when you imitate someone else, you rob the world—and your future—out of the fullness of experiencing you.

Now, look, the human race is about 200,000 years old now, which means that nearly every song or book you get lost in, at least in part, is somewhat of a remix. Which is also to say that radical, unmatched originality is pretty much impossible. We've been bumping up against each other in our creative zones for centuries. I'm certainly not the only writer who's explored the concept and history of a mystical approach to creativity. (Elizabeth Gilbert dives far deeper into it in *Big Magic*, which is a delicious must-read.)

We *depend* upon the ability to toss each other's inspirations around. But blatant imitation of a person's flow or style? It's not cool or flattering. It's icky and violating to the person you're ripping off, and it's disrespectful to your own gifts. It might spawn a flurry of likes on social media initially, but it's not sustainable. Nor is it fulfilling because your higher self will always know the phony game you're playing. When you try to siphon someone else's flavor, and claim it as your own, you rob mankind out of the luxury of experiencing you. And you miss out on juicy, spine-tingling, walking-on-air rendezvous with *your* genius.

As our exploration of what it means to be bravely authentic is drawn to a close, I want you to consider all of the people you've tried to be in your life. In previous chapters, we looked at the labels you've been suppressed by, and, most recently, all of the ways you've tried to mute or shrink your uniqueness in an effort to fit in. But, here, I want you to venture even deeper. I know you ache to build a future that enlists the freedom and joy of honest self-expression. And I know there are people who want and need exactly what only you've got.

So, here are some questions to consider: Has your business not taken off because you've been straight-up copying someone else's model? Do you keep hitting a wall because you're trying to emulate her writing style, even though that's not at all how you talk? Has your art lost its luster because, instead of finding your flow, you're keeping an eye on your competition? Could it be that your relationships feel empty or contrived because you assume that every cozy get-together or glitzy night on the town has to play out in the same cinematic fashion as that of your favorite influencer? Or, maybe that the people you've been doing life with aren't your people, after all?

If so, you might consider inviting the divine to start collaborating with you, even if you're skeptical about the whole idea of a mystical approach to living. You might apologize to your genius for having shoved it to the side so that you could wander down someone else's road. You've got nothing to lose.

There are almost 8 billion people on this planet and none of them see life through the same lens you do. Which means that none of them can collaborate with divinity in the same way you can. I think we can all agree that the last thing this world needs is another reductive version of something or someone it's already seen. So, do us all a favor and let your genius step up to the mic. You're the only version of you we want to meet.

PHASE THREE

LET THE LIGHT &
WONDER IN

MIDPHASE
LOVE NOTE:

The Milky Way galaxy is home
to an astonishing 300 billion stars.

But, you? You're even more abundant and intricate
than the constellations that amaze you and make your
jaw drop to your collarbone.

That heavenly body of yours is home to
seven octillion atoms.

How ravishing and wondrous you are.

RADICAL ACTION:

BUILD A BRAG SANCTUARY

...and make it roar with applause.

How generous we are at echoing back to others their most dazzling accomplishments, yet we often suffer amnesia when remembering our own. We might slip into one creative dry spell and worry that we're doomed to a life of "what might have been," forgetting that we ever made magic at all. Or, we might fear that our best work is behind us, never to join forces with us again.

But what if your most brilliant work is *ahead* of you?

In Madonna's fiery, heart-rending speech at the *Billboard* Women in Music 2016 {34}, she famously reflected upon her early days in New York City, saying, "It was 1979 and New York was a very scary place. In the first year I was held at gunpoint, raped on a rooftop with a knife digging into my throat, and I had my apartment broken into and robbed so many times, I stopped locking the door. In the years that followed, I lost almost every friend I had to AIDS or drugs or gunshots—[I learned] in life there is no real safety except for self-belief."

Self-belief. You can't get anything done in this world without it, yet society often accuses a person of being boastful or narcissistic if they dare to illuminate their own accomplishments or greatness in even subtle ways. We're told to affirm others, but never ourselves. We're told to be humble and levelheaded and modest. But downplaying your strengths is a slap in the face to your creator's handiwork, not yours. It doesn't do anyone any favors. Acknowledging your artistic or intellectual worth isn't gloating; it's not the same thing as believing you're superior to others.

Loving yourself isn't a plight, but a favor to the world. Being vividly awesome doesn't make anyone else less awesome. You're the longest cheerleader you'll ever have. The most tragic loss you could ever experience is the loss of faith in yourself. You've got no more time for minimizing your brilliance and charms. When you stand in your gifts and potential, you show others how to stand in their own. It sends a powerful chain reaction across humanity.

Which brings me to our activity of the hour.

First, I want you to lean into some time travel, calling upon the most noteworthy things you've ever conceptualized or created-the ones that make you stand a bit taller and lift your chin a little higher.

Like, for example, the song lyrics that swarmed everyone in the studio with chills. The silhouette you shaded in art class that your instructor lit up on display. The clever marketing strategy that spawned a stampede of high-fives from your co-workers. The critique you gave to an acquaintance who later said, "You know, that's probably the most helpful feedback I've ever received."

Second, I want you to make a long and lustrous list of the most affirming and scrumptious and uplifting compliments you've ever gotten from those you admire. Our goal here is simple: call upon your most ingenious brain babies, personal victories and zingy endorsements, pausing on the ones that make you buzz with excitement and reconvene with your moxie and prowess.

Once you've taken a 5-star tour of your most proud accomplishments and strokes of genius, relive the glory by covering your board with commemorations of them. Get your emotions involved. This is your self-love altar and you're not allowed to hold back.

Pull the old, coffee-stained movie script from your desk drawer and pin it up somewhere eye-level. Print a photograph of yourself holding the diploma or delivering the sensational performance. Then adorn it with your master list of compliments. Highlight the best ones. Rally for your own greatness-because you now understand that any greatness you carry is actually the greatness of the divine working *through* you.

So don't hold back. Make it roar with applause. Act as your own publicist or stage mom, if that's what does the trick.

Keep your affirmation sanctuary handy and refer to it often, throughout and beyond this program. And, most importantly, let it serve as evidence of what you're capable of doing again, and again, and again...

AFFIRMATION SANCTUARY

MY BRIGHTEST ACCOMPLISHMENTS & MOST UNFORGETTABLE, HEART-SWELLING COMPLIMENTS:

"'WHAT MIGHT
HAVE BEEN'
IS A DREAM
WE PITCH
TO OURSELVES
TO AVOID
BEGINNING AGAIN."

- LACEY JOHNSON
RADICAL LIFE RENOVATION

BEDTIME STORY:

LET LOVE AND MAGIC SHOW UP AS THEY MAY

"Love might land in your orbit in ways that you glance right past, because you're expecting it to align with a specific ideal-maybe one you never really wanted."

I was questioning everything. The love letters by the coffee pot, the romantic weekends spent in dreamy bungalows overlooking the mountains, and the laughing ourselves off of the bed.

We weren't getting pregnant. Months were racing by and becoming years, and the absence was building walls between us. At least from my view. I resented him each time he said, "Just stop worrying about it. Let it happen."

Why was I the only one being pricked with needles and researching the finest fertility teas to drink and praying fervently and speaking all of the mantras into existence? And, if my husband couldn't see how make-or-break this was for me, did he really love me? And, if I was incapable of reproducing, was I even lovable? That's what I often wondered in my darkest hours.

One night, I crawled into bed, alone, trying to envision a future without children. And, while I knew it was my right to grieve the absence of something I desired, I began to realize that, by hinging all of my happiness and lovability on that one thing, I was blinding myself from a myriad of other ways that love had shown up in my life. Somewhere in that space, I let myself remember.

Love was when my dad folded a surprise poem into my school lunch when I was in the sixth grade. On a white piece of paper, in blue ink, he'd written: "A beautiful baby girl was born on August day. When I first saw her, I knew she was perfect in every way…" He underlined every rhyming word.

Love was a rainy August afternoon not long ago. I spotted a man sitting alone at a muddy gravesite along a rural Florida highway. He clutched a red umbrella with one hand and held a sopping wet piece of paper with the other. Everything about the scene reeked of misery, but also beauty. Because, for him to have sacrificed his comfort in that way-muddying up his shoes, enduring the rain as it pounded against his cheeks-could only have been made possible by his love for somebody. And that somebody probably loved him in return.

Love was the back of my friend Sam's head as he searched for our friend Leland's phone on that crisp October day. A few days prior, Leland, one of the sunniest human beings to have ever walked the Earth, had been heartbreakingly killed in a car accident. Some of his belongings were missing, and his dad asked his friends to go to the scene in search of them. None of us necessarily wanted to; those were painfully tainted grounds. Yet, we understood that it was important.

I watched as Sam marched through the tall grass, searching tirelessly. He did it for more than an hour-despite the biting chill in the air, and the cold beer waiting for him in his hotel room, and the patchwork of stains accumulating on his white shoes.

Love was the twinkle in a 95 year-old World War II veteran's eyes when he spoke about meeting his wife after returning from battle. "I met and married my Chloe..." he said. "And, I built her the greenhouse she always wanted." He said her name as though it were a buttery chocolate truffle. And then he showed me the honorable calluses on his hands, cackling proudly.

Love was my mom's brown eyes spilling with tears upon seeing my daughter's nursery having been brought to life. I stood beside her, 8 months pregnant, as she stared in amazement at the dresser stocked full of tiny socks, pink bibs and frilly blankets, and diapers decorated with funny giraffe and elephant patterns.

"I can't believe it..." she whispered, barely able to force the words. "I just can't believe it." To grasp the magnitude of her investment in my joy, understand that she didn't give birth to me. She never fed me a bottle or cheered me on as I took my first, wobbly steps. She married my dad when I was 8 years old-two years after my mother passed away tragically.

Over the years, we've had times of blissful closeness and some of soft distance, mostly because trauma has a way of authoring confusion-causing me to worry if loving her wildly meant rejecting the mother I'd lost. That was until I realized that the two love stories aren't opponents. They can, and absolutely do, co-exist. The truth is, she's a treasure of a bonus mom and a grandmother to my baby girl-one I chose, and who chose me.

I could go on forever, because love shows up when you let yourself see it. Yet, we often expect it to be a series of hair-raising moments. To fit romantically into the contours of society's standards. To render us breathless. But that might not be how it's showing up. I'm not saying you shouldn't have the kind of love you hope for. I've got no interest in challenging your right to grieve the lack of what you desire, should that be the case.

What I'm saying is that love might land in your orbit in ways that you glance right past, because you're expecting it to align with specific ideals-perhaps ones you didn't even create. Perhaps, in some cases, ones you don't *truly* want... and maybe never have.

It was more than four years after I'd begun trying to fill my vacant womb when I stood in my bathroom, clutching a positive pregnancy test in my hand, nearly fainting at the sight of a second line. The room spun. Time stopped. Wars ended. I shouted my husband's name so loudly, the house nearly shook.

Today, we're parents to a dancing, squealing, whip-smart toddler with the sweetest disposition. Also one who cuts her eyes devilishly and shouts orders in our direction from sunrise to sundown. And, yes, through that experience, he's demonstrated his love for me in infinite ways. But our bond as parents isn't the only way his devotion for me blooms. Not at all.

His love announces itself when he protects me from scary movie scenes, whispering, "Baby, just keep your eyes shut. I'll tell you when it's safe to open them." Or the way he lights up when he brews my morning coffee immaculately. I've also realized that my role as a mother, while incomparably edifying, doesn't determine my value as a woman.

Love isn't conceptualized in a Hollywood writing room. It won't always feel like the movies. It sometimes leads us to sit in the pouring rain or get grass stains on our shoes. It's in the highest of highs and in the most disorienting of lows.

But it's also in the unremarkable moments in between.

Maybe you've yet to anchor the cinematic love story you dream about. Or, maybe you ache for children, or for an apology, or for the approval of a parent you never had. If so, I hope those dreams come true for you in time. But, might you zoom in and examine the love you've already got? Might you reflect upon the random instances of favor and serendipity that've drifted into your life?

You know, like the friend who called at the exact moment you felt the most alone. The belated birthday card with a surprise check that landed like a godsend. The cancelled trip that proved to be life-sparing. The times you've said, "If you hadn't shown up, I don't know what I would've done..." The times someone said to you, "It was the weirdest thing, but you were on my heart last night."

For reasons that are too lengthy to unpack in this book (though it's coming in a future one!), I got pregnant at the most magical hour, despite having suffered through four crushing years of infertility. My daughter's conception and birth were eerily supernatural and I'd change nothing about those experiences.

I love her so much it hurts. I'd live through the suffocating pain of infertility all over again, so long as it meant I'd get to be her mother. I've got tears in my eyes right now, as I'm writing this message to you, because I've never meant words more than I mean these.

And yet! The joy I experience as a mother doesn't at all invalidate the despair I felt during those intensely lonely, exasperating years of waiting and wanting. It also doesn't mean I haven't continued to experience hair-yanking frustrations and tribulations on the other side of getting exactly what I asked for.

What I'm saying is that, despite the imperfections and whims and uncertainties of being a human on Earth, divinity has never stopped smiling over me. It's never stopped wooing me and vying for my attention. I truly feel, all the way down in my bones, that God has always been on my side.

Even in stretches of confusion and pain, life has still tossed me beauty and grace and fantastic mystery. Just like it always does. Just like it always will.

So, I bet, if you set aside your blinders of disappointment, and if you invite love to come around as it may, it'll surprise you with how sweetly and often it shows up. Perhaps in ways that'll fill you with warmth and safety.

Maybe even take your breath away...

BEDTIME STORY + RADICAL ACTION:
TRAVEL FAR AND AWAY

How will you ever discover what's truly possible if you never venture beyond your comfy borders?

A young girl fidgeted with her dolls on the kitchen floor, watching her mother pull a leg of ham from a grocery bag and carefully trim an inch off of each end before placing it into a large pan. It was Christmas Eve and the ham was to be drizzled with honey and juices, then baked slowly in the oven all evening long. It would serve as the delectable centerpiece of their family's annual gathering the following day.

"Mommy? Why are you cutting off the ends of the ham like that?" the girl asked. Her mother meandered about the kitchen, wrapping the ham in plastic film and sliding it into a packed refrigerator, battling with overwhelm about all that needed to be accomplished before the doorbell started ringing and guests began trickling into the home.

"Well... sweetie. I'm not sure. It's just how your grandma always prepared it...." she mumbled in response.

"But, why? It looks like there's a lot of meat being thrown into the trash. That's ham we could put on sandwiches later if we-"

"Well, it might help the ham soak up all of the juices or something. You can ask grandma about it tomorrow if you want..." she said, her voice trailing off.

Later that night, after tucking her daughter into bed and arranging a spread of presents around the tree, the mother's curiosity tugged at her. She'd for sure tossed a lot of velvety trimmings into the garbage over the years. The following day, after loved ones began wandering into the foyer and filling their glasses with eggnog and punch, the little girl yanked at her grandma's sweater, asking, "Mommy said you taught her to cut the ends off of the ham before baking it. How come, Grandma? Is it so the meat can soak up the juices better?"

Her grandmother let out a soft chuckle, gently squeezing the young girl's hand. "Well, no, honey, that's not exactly it. You see, when your mother was your age, your grandfather and I didn't have much money. We couldn't afford a bigger pan. Cutting the ham was the only way to make it fit into what we had at the time..."

There've been countless versions of this story retold throughout generations, but the takeaway is crystalline: how might we move about our days doing things we don't have to do, or overlooking things we assume aren't possible-because it's what we've accepted as truth? Might you live your life in ways that are unconsciously wasteful of your precious resources, talents and time? What treasures might you be tossing into the trash?

What if the world as you perceive it isn't entirely real, but a movie projection of the beliefs you inherited? And, if so, you're under no obligation to continue living in a particular version of the world, just because it's the one that was handed to you.

A few years ago, I interviewed Dr. Deepak Chopra for a magazine cover story {35} in support of his book, *You Are the Universe* {36}. We chatted about paradigms, which he said are "self-fulfilling." Going back to the opening chapter of this book, where we examined the lies you've been subconsciously obeying as truth throughout your life, each of us are programmed by a series of experiences, impressions and indoctrinations from early childhood, which then knits together our individual paradigm-a fixed set of thought patterns and concepts that we operate from all day long, mostly on autopilot. Most of us are oblivious to how confining and limiting our paradigm is. As we explored in the first chapter, sometimes many of the beliefs in our paradigm are downright cruel.

You might compare your paradigm to a fun house with mirrors that distort your perceptions of the world at every turn-exaggerating some aspects of truth and shrinking others, all the while keeping you trapped inside, unable to find your way out without growing dizzy and uncomfortable. So, then, how might you escape it, or, perhaps, get a glimpse of what exists beyond it? The answer is both simple and extreme: radically new information. In *You Are the Universe*, Dr. Chopra calls this a "jumping out" process.

There were so many delicious takeaways from our conversation, but here are the most memorable (the last of which is so fundamentally, hilariously, earth-shatteringly brilliant):

- "The human universe is created in human consciousness, and mine is not the same as yours. The world as you know it is not quite the same world as I know it."

- Through [your desire for transcendence] you can gradually begin to loosen the hold of your conceptual frameworks, which are programmed through your conditioning. This conceptual framework comes from literally centuries of conditioning, which are formed through the repetition of prior conditioning processes. They come from parents, religion, culture, economics and personal experiences.

- "The dog in the White House doesn't know he's in the White House, or that his label is 'dog'..."

So, might you consider this: the world you call home-from the disk-shaped structure of the Milky Way to Earth's coral reefs and painted deserts and spewing volcanoes and underwater waterfalls-what if you're not entirely a product of it, but a co-author in it? What if it's all so amazingly within your reach?

Which is also to say, what if you're not merely being shuffled and spun through life's frames, funneled helplessly through its light and darkness, possibilities and restrictions, happenstances and vagaries, but a co-director in your own movie? Which brings me to the action prompt of the hour.

Tonight, as you float toward slumber, I want you to ask yourself, "Starting tomorrow, how might I venture out of my norm and follow the melody of my curiosities? How might I begin 'jumping out' of the confines of my morning, afternoon and nightly routines?"

Don't overthink this. It simply involves traveling beyond your habits and ideologies-perhaps even stretching beyond your social constructs. It's about delighting yourself with things outside of your routine-perhaps things you've long been curious about. Whether it be ordering toasted challah and eggs for breakfast instead of your usual banana nut muffin, or soaking up a subculture or an era that intrigues you, it's about giving yourself a glimpse of what exists beyond the life you walk around in everyday-beyond the fashions and languages and scenery and zip codes that are most familiar. Even if it feels intimidating at first.

Let's say, for example, you've long dreamt of traveling to Europe, yet never believed the trip was doable, financially or logistically. You might start by creating a Pinterest board with breathtaking panoramas that beckon for adventure. Or, you could log onto Google Earth and wander down the cobblestone streets of Paris or explore the sun-washed landscapes of the Amalfi Coast, letting yourself get a feel for the sights and sounds.

As you engage in explorations like these, your reticular activating system (RAS), an extraordinarily important network of neurons in your brain stem that facilitate stimuli, such as arousing action and filtering out the things you not only perceive, but nod "yes" and "no" to (I promise we'll dive deeper into the RAS and how to make yours work in your favor in a later chapter), will begin to gradually shift {37}. This'll allow your brain to vividly "see" the quest as no longer being something you'd love to experience in a distant lifetime, but something that's within your reach. Maybe even something that's already underway.

Another idea is to venture to an unfamiliar nook of your city or town. You could visit a corner café with a spread of buttery croissants or delectable truffles you've never tasted, or slide on a shimmering dress and score tickets for a theatre you've never visited.

Or, you could wander into a comedy show or poetry reading on a street you've never crossed, or take a scenic hike-traversing through cactus gardens you've never thought to pause and photograph and marvel at. Perhaps you live an afternoon drive away from a nature trail or a museum you've never thought to investigate, but might fall in love with.

There's also time travel-my personal favorite. For this, you call to mind an era that's long intrigued you, immersing your curiosities into its customs, dialects, fashions, music and slang. This might involve sinking into a rapturous novel that encapsulates the essence of its energy and style, or binge-watching a television series like *The Mary Tyler Moore Show*, *Bridgerton* or *Little Fires Everywhere*, or a movie like *Casablanca*. You could head to the library and thumb through archived news clippings that offer a glimpse into the era's heroes, icons, renegades and revolutions.

However you wish to uniquely interpret this is perfect-because that's the point. Just let yourself be blissfully transported away from your daily life. Give yourself permission to venture beyond the paradigm that you inherited.

The idea here isn't to escape or deny your reality, but to become enchanted and stretched by unfamiliar experiences so that you can *expand* upon your reality. Because, again, when you introduce fresh flavors, textures and visuals to your brain, it'll begin operating from a much broader map-one that's designed with possibility and revolution.

The world is vast, but it's also small. And your universe is not the same one as mine. When you stretch and reorder your consciousness, you alter the entire universe as you know it. Something that feels impossible right now might be entirely-(perhaps, humorously)- possible, so long as you're willing to make way for the strange and far-fetched to drift into your atmosphere.

So, introduce yourself to something fantastically intriguing and peculiar today. Because, eventually, it might become so wonderfully breezy and familiar.

Just like that unrecognizable reality you want to step into so badly, it hurts.

ERAS, PEOPLE, PLACES & THINGS...

I FEEL DRAWN TO EXPLORE, TRY OR VISIT, BUT HAVEN'T (YET):

A LIST OF DELIGHTFUL AND INTERESTING WAYS I MIGHT "JUMP OUT" OF MY DAILY RESTRICTIONS & ROUTINES:

BEDTIME STORY + RADICAL ACTION:

GIVE SOME LIFE AWAY AND LET IT BURN

*...because the real transformation begins
when you let your love and light take center stage.*

We live in a world of being glued to our screens. Of sponsored posts and splashy influencer opportunities. You can't scroll through your social media apps without comparing yourself to someone else's glamorized, over-filtered sub-reality, or without being seduced by a "swipe up."

There's so much effort to persuade and convince-so much of doing things to draw attention or snag followers and shares. Might that play a role in why, even prior to surviving a global pandemic, we've been becoming an increasingly anxious, depressed and lonely society? Suicide rates are at an astonishing high, and is now the second leading cause of death among young people {38}. So, how might we cure this epidemic? How might we access genuine connection-the kind that flourishes without expectation and glory?

Enter altruism. Studies show that giving from a place of sheer, unselfish love and humanity sparks feelings of purpose, and helps us transcend our own suffering. In fact, research from The Cleveland Clinic shows that giving is so overwhelmingly therapeutic to our health, it can lower blood pressure, inspire self-worth, take the edge off of depression and anxiety, and potentially extend your life {39}.

Have you ever felt what's called the "helper's high"? It's the rush of euphoria that follows a generous deed {40}. It might feel as though you're gliding along in the arms of divinity, swaying with a beam of light and love, in a dance with all of humankind. But, intoxicating as it may be, its scientific explanation is simple: giving activates areas of your brain that are linked to pleasure, trust and connection, flooding your bloodstream with a juicy cocktail of feel-good chemicals like serotonin, dopamine and oxytocin. This means that, if ever you feel like you can't take anymore of whatever it is your exhausted heart and mind are tired of dragging along, slip into a spirt of giving.

I learned this lesson a little more than a decade ago, when I spent two summers in Belize. Not the tourist-driven Belize you might be thinking of, though. My Belize, the one I know and treasure infinitely, is along the dirt paths that are seldom photographed. Under the avocado and cashew trees. Where I spent long hours nearly fainting from the sweltering sun.

Where there was no running water, I found God. But, before I go on, let me back up and explain how I arrived there.

While in college, studying and preparing for my future journalism career, I worked as a traveling makeup artist for a well-known cosmetic brand. I filled in eyebrows and painted smoky eyes for both fancy and small events. It was a fun and character-building time in my life, but the most rewarding part was the indispensable connections I occasionally formed with strangers.

Though the majority of customers may have wandered into my makeup chair to learn how to lengthen their eyelashes or accentuate their cheekbones, we often traveled to more essential places. I'd listen as they unpacked their regrets about the past and insecurities about the present, and entertained their dreams for the future. I fell in love with the way their eyes lit up anytime I awakened a rare and beautiful part of them that they'd never seen.

One sunny April Saturday, a petite woman with strawberry blonde hair collapsed into my chair. "I wasn't planning on doing this today. I just got off of a plane..." she said, her voice trailing off breathlessly, while tossing a pile of shopping bags to the side.

Her name was Connie and I felt an immediate, inexplicable connection with her. She told me she'd spent the previous two weeks in Belize. She and her husband headed a mission trip there twice a year, concentrating on the villages with the most urgent needs. They built havens for families who were on the edge of homelessness, and offered free medical and dental care for everyone in the community, and entertained the children with puppet shows. But they weren't there to act as "saviors." Their aim was to build sincere, lasting relationships, cultivate spiritual healing and serve as living, breathing examples of hope and humanity.

Instantaneously, something lit up inside of me, flashing with authority, commanding my attention. I'd felt trapped in one of the lowest, most mind-numbing stretches of my life and was frantically searching for a way to squirm out of it. It was as though there was a gravitational pull between the parts of me that were on the verge of spiritual decay and the sign-up sheet for the next trip. As though I was being guided by my soul's GPS system.

"Oh! I'd love to learn more about this! I've been looking for something like this to involve myself with!" I gushed. The words spilled from my mouth so fast, I didn't have a chance to tuck them back in.

"Oh, really?" she asked, surprised. "Well, we're usually booked by now, but we just had someone cancel today. We've got one slot left for the trip in June."

Minutes later, I was jotting down all of the sign-up details onto the back of a skincare pamphlet. And, two months later, I was boarding a plane for Belize City with 40 people I'd never met, my heart thumping with anticipation and nervousness.

Yet, through every disconcerting motion, I knew, without reservation, that I was exactly where I was meant to be. I knew that every decision leading up to that moment couldn't have been more providential. Still, I had no way of knowing that, two weeks after that, I'd be dragging my luggage through baggage claim, dreading the moment I'd greet the concrete and reconvene with my city-realizing that I'd undergone a metamorphosis so uncomfortably irreversible, I didn't have the language to unpack it for anyone. Including myself.

I hadn't wanted to leave that paradise and return to my privileged, air-conditioned life with my entitled, bullying, possessive boyfriend and our vapid conversations. Or certain aspects of my job that suddenly seemed hollow and superficial. I'd fallen in love with moving about my days in a spirit of selflessness and unity. It was the happiest, most whole I'd felt since I was a child.

Whether taking blood pressures or temperatures, or running errands for the nurses, or hauling materials across the construction site, or playing games with the children, I felt like I'd been hanging out on God's front porch steps, soaking up a sunrise of a lifetime. Each of those families and children cracked me open and exposed me to parts of myself that I'd desperately needed to see. In turn, they gave me more than I ever gave them-etching their joy and gratitude and perspective on my heart in a way that'll remain intact until I'm a pile of bones.

So, today I ask that you begin to think of ways you might contribute to someone else's comfort, healing, safety or welfare. This can be carried out in a myriad of ways, and the only rule is that you act from a place that has no concern for what you might get in return. For example, you could thumb through your closets and gather stacks of blankets and coats you haven't used in years. You could clean them and fold them lovingly and prayerfully, then venture over to your local donation center. Or, perhaps, blast out an energetic email, asking to be put in the way of whomever might need bedding or warm clothing.

Or, you could offer your blood or plasma, then light a candle and spend an hour in reverent silence, honoring whomever's life you might've saved. You could visualize for them years of charming hikes and belly laughs and enriching, pain-free experiences with their loved ones. Our society might be one that's competing and self-seeking, but the transcendence everyone is searching for is in the giving. The kind that doesn't ask to be documented or to hook followers.

Last year, after having been a guest on her podcast, *Minding the Mental Mess* {41}, I interviewed Dr. Caroline Leaf, a remarkably insightful and passionate neuroscientist, and author of *Cleaning Up Your Mental Mess* (amongst a stack of other brilliant bestsellers), for an *O, the Oprah Magazine* (now *Oprah Daily*) story {42}. When asked about the less-obvious ways to cultivate intimacy in relationships, along with how one might mend a wounded ability to trust, she shouted the power of giving, suggesting that doing so will serve to bring restoration and richness to one's future.

"As a person works to heal and rebuild their own identity, it's vital for them to reach out and actively do things to enhance the lives of others. Sharing and caring activates beautifully coordinated waves of energy in the brain, and, by default, automatically enhances the giver's life experiences, making them more resilient and helping them discover re-conceptualized ways of moving forward," she said.

I love this so much because I've lived it. I know the power it carries. Without knowing the magnitude of what I was doing at the time, I experienced this alchemy firsthand. I learned that giving days and weeks of my life away to others could help me save and rehabilitate my own.

So, tonight and tomorrow and from here on out, let your love and light take center stage. Give it flavors or textures or hands or the contents of your closet or whatever else you might have to offer. Then give it away and let it burn through the darkness and suffering, more and more each time.

THESE ARE THE WAYS I MOST FEEL LED TO GIVE OF MY EXPERTISE, HEART, TALENTS AND TIME...

PHASE THREE

MY MOST POWERFUL REVELATIONS
DURING THIS PHASE HAVE BEEN...

PHASE THREE

RADICAL DAILY 4 CHECK-IN:

ANY HOPE REKINDLED? INTERESTS REDISCOVERED?
VICTORIES WON (BIG OR SMALL)?

"ANYTHING THAT WORKS AGAINST YOU CAN ALSO WORK FOR YOU ONCE YOU UNDERSTAND THE PRINCIPLE OF REVERSE."

- MAYA ANGELOU
I KNOW WHY THE CAGED BIRD SINGS

PHASE FOUR

BUILD A
BEAUTIFUL FUTURE:

to courageously and determinedly build a stairway
between what is and what's desired, so that you
can finally step into the version of yourself that
you've been dreaming about for way too long;

to embrace that you're the co-creator in every
frame of your life, and to decide how you're going
to show up within each of them,
no matter what comes your way;

and, finally, to allow the beautiful movie to unfold-
not just in your daydreams, in your promises
or on your vision board,
but in your reality.

WHERE THERE'S FIRE, THE CRIPPLED RUN

...because urgency is an elixir of miracles.

When my great-grandmother, Ida, was in her 60s, she developed progressive supranuclear palsy, a disease of the nervous system that caused her to fall backward anytime she walked. A year or so after her diagnosis, she'd been resigned to a life in a wheelchair.

By then, she could take no more than a few wobbly steps at a time, and only if someone was holding her torso upright. Sadly, this meant she was forced to pack up all of her cookware and keepsakes from her beloved abode, where she'd once spent afternoons combing through thorny bushes and filling baskets with plump, juicy blackberries in a nearby field. She'd have to move in with her daughter and son-in-law (my maternal grandparents), because living alone was no longer an option.

Once she was settled comfortably into her new arrangement, my grandparents began leaving her alone for several hours at a time each weekday, in order to operate their auto service shop a few miles away. One day, my grandparents retreated home for a quick lunch, as they often did. But, on this day, their phones began ringing with a slew of customer requests, causing them to rush through their meal and scrape their dirty plates in a frenzy.

An hour or so after the house had fallen quiet and the afternoon sun had come pouring in, Ida relaxed into her wheelchair, in front of her bedroom television set, cross-stitching and soaking up her favorite soap operas. Suddenly, she smelled something burning. A sick feeling swarmed her.

In a panic, she tossed her wheels forward, racing down the hallway and swinging left into the kitchen. To her horror, there were flames rising from an iron skillet on the stove. A cloud of smoke billowed wildly above it. She rushed toward the flames, grabbing the skillet handle and tossing it into the sink. But the fire caught the edge of a curtain. Instantaneously, the flames began crawling up the wall. Seconds later, Ida found herself pacing along the front porch, her feet stomping against the cement, wagging her arms, yelling, "Help! Help! There's a fire!" She then rushed back inside and yanked the portable phone from the wall, frantically dialing my grandmother's work line, still on her feet as confidently as anyone had ever been.

Shortly thereafter, the fire department came rushing into the driveway, trailed by my grandparents. They grabbed their hoses and extinguished the blaze quickly. For weeks after, my family was aghast. How had my severely crippled great-grandmother not only stood upright, and not only taken steps on her own, but had darted in and out of the house with the spunk and sprightliness of a child? Even she couldn't explain what her body had done.

You've probably heard stories of various inexplicable events like this one. Like, say, the 110-pound mother who lifts up an SUV with her bare hands in order to rescue her child from danger. Science offers droves of evidence about adrenaline, endorphins and other chemical releases surging humans with supernatural pain relief and vigor. But my take is that there's an earth-shatteringly simple explanation: urgency is an elixir of miracles.

Here's what I believe: If ever you want to make magic happen in your life, leap into an inferno of urgency. Act like your life is catching fire. Because, whether or not you can smell it burning, it is.

If you're tired of feeling like you're flunking Earth-of not doing what you swear you're going to do, of not paying your bills on time, of not opening your eyes each morning with a spirit of gratitude and purpose, of not finalizing your business plan, of not being attentive and loyal to the ones you love, swing open a window of urgency.

You don't have the promise of tomorrow. None of us do. That's an illusion we love to tote around throughout life, and we're then gutted when the illusion is shattered. Today could be your last day as an accountant, or a chef, or a YouTube influencer or a stay-at-home mom. It could be the last time you fill your coffee cup or press your lips against your child's forehead. The last time you blow out your birthday candles. The last time you gut-laugh with your best friend. The last opportunity to make amends. Maybe you've got five more decades ahead of you, but you've got no way of knowing for sure.

Someday someone is going to come behind you and sift through your drawers and private folders, and maybe sob into their hands as they replay your voice messages and reread your texts. All that you ever did will become the story of you. There'll be no chance to make a single edit. Not one. So, then, what do you want your legacy to be? How do you want your future grandchildren to describe you to their friends, should you have them? How do you want your obituary to read? This is reason to be urgently excited. Urgently curious and kind and seeking and hopeful and present and willing.

Can you imagine what you might accomplish if you'd wake up from your dream of false comfort and complacency, and let yourself feel the sting of urgency? Your life is not some silly toss-away idea whipping through the wind; it's a hugely miraculous mega-deal.

Have you ever noticed how the most unmotivated people-the ones who behave like entitled, helpless children long into adulthood-often have the most abundant resources available to them? Here's why: someone is always rescuing them, so they've got no incentive to rescue themselves.

There's always someone sealing their leaks, satisfying their debts, replacing their tires, glossing over their mistakes, explaining away their mishaps. They never shine on their own because they don't have to. They've never been tossed into the furnace of "figure it out," which means they've never danced with urgency, which means they've never built any confidence or character or grit. So, while society loves to point fingers at people like this, scoffing at their perceived laziness and lack of motivation, the truth is that, oftentimes, their idleness comes from never having been conditioned to believe in themselves.

But, you know what would be so profoundly miraculous for a person like this? The terrifyingly scorching gift of urgency. If they were shoved into its flames and forced to become so uncomfortable that they had no choice but to hunt their way out of danger, so to speak, they'd finally have a chance to realize their potential. It'd be the most life-unlocking handout anyone ever gave them.

Tremendous research shows that the key to setting a child up for success-whatever that might mean for them-is to sit back and allow them to fail every now and then {43}. Which means that, if they know no one's coming to save them from their mishap or sticky predicament, they better learn how to save themselves. They better figure out how to worm their way out of said failure. Urgently.

As you drift to dreams tonight, I ask that you steep on the concept of urgency. There's a gift in every crisis, an embrace in every rejection, and a sloppy, wet kiss in every obstacle. It means you're being hurled into the flames of renovation-because that's how capable and resilient you are. It means you're being given an opportunity to forge authentic confidence-something no one else is capable of giving to you.

I can't predict what your next right move should be. I can't promise that heartache or misfortune won't find you again. But allow me to remind you that if you're reading this, you're still breathing. You've still got space to fill between your dash. You're not forgotten. Which means you're being urgently invited to be a participant on this planet. So, no matter what's crippled you in your life, accept no more bail-outs. Make no more excuses. Nix the laziness and imposter syndrome and victim rhetoric. Stop feeling sorry for yourself and start remembering how powerful you are.

Stand before every tomorrow as though it's the only one you've got left. Because it might be. Then run and leap toward your dreams like your life is catching fire. Because it is.

BEDTIME STORY + RADICAL ACTION:

IF THE DREAM PERSISTS, STOP DIGGING ITS GRAVE

If you don't take full, courageous responsibility for your own happiness, who will?

One October afternoon a few years ago, one of my girlfriends and I made the hour-long drive from Nashville to an old cemetery in Adams, Tennessee. The town is famous for its dark and witchy past, and is rumored to be haunted at every hillside. And, while I'm certainly not a fan of gruesome folklore, supernatural fare always gets me jazzed. I'm drawn to the things that can't be unpacked in practical terms. I'm the girl who'll gather an entourage of paranormal enthusiasts around the dinner table just to compare goosebumps.

But, while most people consider old graveyards to be creepy and somber, I actually think they're fascinating-perhaps electrifying. If that lands a bit weird to you, let me explain. When I see old tombstones, I don't see death per se; I see graduates. It's a feeling of deep, spacious reverence. It's like standing before a sea of stories and collecting evidence of those who've completed their earthly assignment, while knowing that I'm still floating somewhere in the beginning, middle or end of mine.

Every marked grave is a record of a first cry and a final breath. Every buried body, having since become a pile of bones, was once housed by the safety of its mother's womb. So much anticipation and love and hope for the future, which then became a unique collective of desires, heartbreaks, confusions, griefs, regrets, epiphanies, splendors, passions, promises and memories. And then the music stopped.

Les Brown famously said, "The graveyard is the richest place on earth, because it is here that you will find all the hopes and dreams that were never fulfilled..." I've been haunted by this quote since I first heard it years ago. And I've come to experience cemeteries as being ripe and abundant grounds, specifically because humans have a history of hauling their dearly beloved aspirations and unborn desires to the grave with them. So, while exploring the cemetery with my friend that day, she may've been hunting for ghostly sightings or hankering for a chill down her spine, but there were other things tugging at my hair. I was too riveted by the peculiarity of it all-that I was almost certainly in the company of unwritten books and love letters, untried inventions, unsung songs, unpainted canvases, unspoken apologies, and volumes of untapped potential. And no telling what else.

In Bronnie Ware's bestselling memoir, *The Top Five Regrets of the Dying: A Life Transformed By the Dearly Departing* {44}, which was inspired by her eight years of working in palliative care, she revealed that, in her experience, the number one regret of people on their deathbed is this: "I wish I'd had the courage to live a life true to myself, not the life others expected of me."

I've made similar observations. Since I was a child, I've loved exploring the minds of more seasoned humans. If you're 70 and above, I probably want to take a stroll through your brain. I'm a junkie for even the most unremarkable stories. And, always, on the other side of every starry-eyed string of questioning, I've noticed a recurring theme–one that defies gender, personality and privilege: there's almost always something unfinished that the person wishes they'd done.

Some have entire novels or screenplays they wish they'd written. Opportunities they wish they'd grabbed. Possibilities they wish they'd anchored. Moves or travels they wish they'd made. There's almost always a laundry list of legitimate reasons why a particular dream was never pursued, but it doesn't change the way they feel: regretful. I can always sense a flicker of grief about what they almost created or said or explored, but didn't.

This sickens me. And, yet, we keep repeating ourselves. We keep postponing and procrastinating and self-sabotaging. And it's entirely understandable, right? Life presents distractions and storm clouds at random junctures and turns, for everyone. No one's story is without a demon of sorts to wrestle. But, ultimately, our will determines who wins.

Here's what I want you to think deeply about, as you drift to dreams tonight: So long as you're still of sound mind and of full breath, and so long as you're not on your deathbed, how badly do you want the things you keep on dreaming about? How badly do you not want to haul your most dearly beloved aspirations to the grave with you? Are you willing to draw your swords of faith and self-determination in order to duel for your own creative and intellectual and spiritual urges?

Year after year, you've said you're going to do it. You scribble the reminders in your planner. You make the New Year's resolutions. You cut out images from magazines and splatter them across your vision board. You might watch others from afar, internally screaming, "She's living my life! That's what I want! That's supposed to be MY life!" And, year after year, there's this little flicker inside that just won't burn out. No matter how many times doubt has tried to hiss a little louder than desire, it fails.

You want it. You know you want it. You yearn for it all the way down in the hollows of your bones. And, somehow, you believe it's possible. For the love of God, even if in some alternate, upside-down universe, it's so fantastically possible.

Sometimes, in your mind's eye, it feels so close, it's like you could step inside the party at any moment. You can almost feel the music thumping and hear the glasses clicking from a nearby room. But you don't take the necessary steps to get there. You don't take full, courageous responsibility for your own happiness. After months or years, you still haven't. Why?

I think the problem with most of us dreamers is that we've been taught to avoid pain and discomfort at any cost. We might want our glory day, sure, but not to the same degree that we want to avoid the sting of judgment or rejection. For whatever reason, most dreamers shiver at the idea of what might be on the other side of their comfort zone.

Instead of taking consistent, disciplined action, they allow that beautiful dream to dangle just out of reach. They keep it close and lukewarm, but at a safe distance, telling themselves and others that they'll get to it "someday."

But too many of us live as though we've got the promise of thousands of tomorrows, though not a single one of us does. That's why I think "someday" is one of the most tragic words in the English language. It's a seductive death sentence to our dreams, and I try to avoid saying it at all anymore. No one ever did the world-or themselves-any favors by running on a loop of false promises, avoidance and procrastination.

So, when it comes to a desire that's been lighting up your heart, year after year, begging to be given life, I want you to replace "someday" with "right now," "as soon as possible" or "in progress." Starting this minute. Otherwise you're slowly digging its grave.

DREAMS I'VE BEEN NEGLECTING

BEDTIME STORY:

SUCCESS IS SELF-ANOINTED

If you want it badly enough, you'll create a way.

On an early spring afternoon in 1989, 20-year-old Daymond John paced along the pavement outside of the Colosseum Mall, on the corner of 165th Street and Jamaica Avenue in Queens, New York. Examining his wad of cash, he thumbed through the crumpled bills, counting them and smoothing them out slowly, disbelieving that he'd turned a modest $40 fabric purchase (funded by long hours spent on his feet, ringing up crispy chicken orders at a local fast-food restaurant and busing tables at a Red Lobster), into a stunning $800 profit.

The week prior, he'd spent his hours curled over a sewing machine in his mom's basement, designing hats to sell to the kids in his neighborhood. Ones he had no idea if anyone would like. But, as it turned out, people did like them. Lots of people. And he realized he was onto something.

Raised by a single mother in Queens, and having become the man of his household at the age of 10, money was an elusive concept. The funds for college for sure weren't there, so that wasn't on his radar. And, to further shrink his scope of opportunities, he'd been diagnosed with Dyslexia. Still, there was one thing he knew he had dominion over: his mind. He wouldn't let his hardships define him or quell his self-belief.

His mother had instilled in him the ethos that, just because golden opportunities weren't bumping up against him or tugging at his sleeve didn't mean they weren't spinning in his orbit. John would just have to reach higher in order to anchor them down. He'd have to experiment and retool, and, eventually, create an opportunity he could monetize. And, in the years that followed, his strategy worked, to put it modestly.

John's venue upgraded from neighborhood street corners to massive trade show booths to an extravagant office in the Empire State Building. His makeshift hat business became FUBU, an explosively popular, multi-million dollar clothing line that defined Hip Hop culture in the 90s and early 2000s. His designs became hot commodities on MTV. He dined with then-president Bill Clinton at the White House. And, decades later, at the time of this writing, the 52-year-old is a multi-millionaire investor and fan favorite on ABC's *Shark Tank*, a bestselling author and one of the most Googled businessmen in the world.

So how did he do it? What was his secret formula?

That's what I wanted to find out a few years ago when I was editor-in-chief of *The Connect*, an inspired living and entrepreneurship magazine, and interviewed John for a cover story {45}. During our hour-long phone conversation, he spoke candidly about his early FUBU days, when he was denied 27 bank loan applications, thus propelling his mother to take out a second mortgage on her house, and turn her basement into a Hip Hop apparel factory.

He revealed how, in those early days, nearly every waking hour that was not spent tying himself into his Red Lobster uniform and serving biscuits was spent designing, sewing, boxing up orders and patrolling night clubs in hopes of getting the apparel into the hands of influential people.

But here's the part I admire most: once he started turning a real profit, he didn't burn his Red Lobster uniform and pop bottles of champagne with his friends and book a flight to Mexico so that he could nap on the beach for two weeks. Instead, he kept clocking in. Even after his designs were being paraded around by LL Cool J. Even after orders were spilling out of his answering machine all day long, he kept counting his tips and strategizing about how to pour every dollar back into his fledging dream.

Here's what I've come to believe, having now interviewed a hefty volume of accomplished and celebrated human beings: the hallmark of a successful person is a marriage of two unglamorously stubborn things: a ravenous desire to contribute and a cemented belief in their own resilience. Whether by way of art or literature or technology, the successful person has decided to be an active participant on Earth. For them, it's not about scaling to the top of the mountain and collapsing once they've reached their destination on high. Instead, they're constantly pregnant with new and innovative ways to lend their gifts to mankind. And, though they might bend, and take a stretch of rest, they'll never let an obstacle break them.

During our interview, there was something John said that I've since folded into all of my aspirations. While unpacking the process of authoring his book, *Rise and Grind* {46}, I asked him how it felt to have employed hundreds of people over the years–people who'd been able to provide nice homes for their families and send their kids to top-ranking schools. John said he was most proud of how he'd sort of helped rewrite the storyline for some of those families, perhaps generationally.

Then, after a pause, he said this: "I've never made anybody successful, though. I've given them opportunities, but I didn't make anybody successful. People can only ever make themselves successful..."

.

I love that so much, it almost makes me want to leap and twirl around my living room Because, when it comes to luck, I don't believe truer words were ever spoken. When it comes to luck, sometimes the only way is to create your own.

Please don't misunderstand me. I know that biases and hardships and traumas and injustices are undeniably, woefully real. I'll never denounce or minimize anyone's pain or struggle, or claim to understand their experience for a second. But, I want you to think about this: someone might have exceptional talent and boundless financial resources and unending parental support and smashing good looks, yet never contribute anything of value to themselves or the world.

Yet, there are those, like Daymond John, who barrel through hardships and setbacks with focus and grit, letting their hunger lead them. These are the people who create an explosively brilliant life for themselves-one that blesses so many others.

Because success is always self-anointed.

You can offer someone all of the backing and funding and scholarships and pep talks they'll ever need, but if they won't get out of bed, or turn down the party invitation, or have the humility to learn from their errors and readjust accordingly, or search for a window when met with a slamming door, success won't come. Or, at least, it for sure won't last.

My wise friend and most called-upon expert, Dr. Kevin Gilliland, clinical psychologist, founder of Innovation360 and guiding light of mental health, recently said to me in an interview, "There's always an element of choice. With emotional scars, you can make wonderful things."

And that's just the truth.

So, if you want to be successful, whether it be in your personal relationships or in your beloved vocation, you'll find a way. You'll overturn every stone until you've discovered all that you're capable of achieving and contributing.

You'll fumble, and cry, and scream into your pillow, and get back up, and refine your strategy a hundred times, and, through that jagged process, anoint yourself.

BUILD A BEAUTIFUL FUTURE

MIDPHASE
LOVE NOTE:

Anytime you feel low, think of something you love.

Like the afternoon sun pouring through the lush, summer trees. A calm, quiet house just after dawn. Flushed cheeks in the fall. The smell of old books. A massage that hits just right. A warm, sincere hug. The sight of puppies squirming and stretching and waking from slumber.

And, then remember: for everything you love, there's yet another example of why
there's so incredibly much to love about you.

BEDTIME STORY:

WHY YOUR OVERSTRESSED BRAIN NEEDS GOOD NEWS, ALWAYS

...but only if you wish to direct the future in your favor.

At the dawn of the COVID era, during quarantine, I took to my Instagram stories, confessing to all who'd listen, "It's a crazy time to be a member of the media right now. Nearly every page or video I stumble upon, someone is spewing their hatred for reporters and news sources."

With my 1 year-old daughter tumbling over my chest and tugging at my hair, I begged, "Most journalists are in this position because they genuinely care about the truth-and they care about delivering it to you. I know we're in a frustrating time, but please stop blaming the media." I'd seek comfort in Zoom chats with my girlfriends, but that only seemed to aggravate my frustration. After the light-hearted banter and updates were exchanged, someone would inevitably toss out a comment like, "Well, I'm not buying what they're selling..." or "The media is spinning it, of course..."

As though "the media" were a band of cruel and twisted gods all huddled in a corner, wiggling their fingers and exchanging wicked grins, getting their rocks off by swindling the world into isolation. I wanted to reach through my screen, thump each of them on the nose and beg, "For the love of God, do you realize who you're talking to? Please stop disparaging the messengers!"

Those were discombobulating days. Like so many others, my once-peaceful home life was suddenly in a tizzy. As more warehouses padlocked their doors, my husband was left grappling with panic about what was to come of his transportation company. And, in between sanitizing groceries, breastfeeding, changing poopy diapers and wiping applesauce from my daughter's chin, I was frantically hustling to meet a slew of deadlines that covered timely topics in the realm of "how to talk to your kids about the coronavirus" and "how to safely date during COVID."

I took that responsibility extraordinarily seriously. Desperate as I was to illuminate the truth for those who doubted the seriousness of the virus, sensationalism was never my goal. Still, as the days stretched on, and as social distractions were stripped away from us, and the pulse of life continuously slowed, I couldn't help but pay attention in a way I'd never paid attention before.

When there's no chatty Happy Hour to dash off to, no perfume aisle to stroll, no sweaty, swaying bodies surrounding you at a concert, no pedicure chair to sink into and no coffee shop conversations to eavesdrop, you start to notice things you didn't notice before. Suddenly, there was a huge magnifying mirror being held in front of all of our faces. About ourselves. About our relationships. About our habits and vices and priorities. About how and where we channeled our energy, day to day.

The truth is, while I absolutely love being a journalist and know that I was made for this role, and while I continue to believe that the vast majority of my colleagues carry out their duties with integrity, I began to realize some of my industry's shadow aspects in a way I'd never paid mind before.

The breaking news headlines that glowed from my phone screen all hours of the day were fueling my anxieties like crazy. The feature stories and somber opinion pieces that accompanied them injected me with dread and hopelessness. As though the reports were vultures and my emotions were prey. Soon, I couldn't deny what I needed to do in order to preserve my mental health, as soon as possible. The *New York Times* push notifications had to go, at least for a while. Then *BuzzFeed*. Then about two dozen accounts I'd been following on Instagram.

Because, while blind living wasn't a stance I wanted to take, the doom-filled forecasts were making me physically ill. I needed a reason to celebrate like I needed air and water.

So, if you can relate-if you ever feel as though you're in a battle between wanting to stay informed and wanting to ditch the news and social media altogether, this chapter is a significant one for you. I'm going to unpack the science behind why tuning your brain to hopeful, uplifting information is not only healthy, but essential to the future you're in the process of building. Also why being a passionate seeker of good news isn't at all living blindly, but intelligently. Because the truth of what you feed your mind will absolutely become the truth of your life.

A few months ago, I led a coaching call on mindset renovation for a fairly large group of women entrepreneurs. I unpacked my journey of personal reinvention a decade ago, confessing that, when I became a more compassionate and gracious screenwriter, as well as a more disciplined director, in the story of my own life, everything changed for the better-the emotional arcs, the lucky breaks, the scenery, the plot twists, the quality of cast members. All of it.

A slew of listeners leaned into their screens, buzzing with the same questions: "But *how* do you learn to think new thoughts? How do you change your beliefs? How do you make a lasting change to your mindset-enough for it to make a real difference in your life?"

The answer is so earth-shatteringly simple, few ever apply it. You take absolute dominion over the data you feed to your mind. You become a cheerfully vigilant, micromanaging CEO of the content you consume. You act as your mind's shielding, unduly attentive and loving housemother. Every single day. In all of the ways.

Here's why: your brain is so powerful, if you think about it often enough, you'll probably get it.

In our digital age, we sift through billions of bits of data while sipping our morning latte or zig-zagging through traffic. And somehow, miraculously, we never short circuit. Instead, we prioritize the onslaught of images and impressions that rush toward us. Which means some things hit us like a flashing billboard and others drift right over our heads, going totally unnoticed.

In an earlier chapter, I touched on the function of the The Reticular Activating System (RAS), which is responsible for this process. To refresh your memory, it's a bundle of nerves at your brainstem that filters out certain information and allows other information to slide on through. It's a pretty remarkable system when you think about it.

I'll give you a simple example of your RAS at work. Let's say you land a fancy job offer in Arizona. You don't have any friends or family who live there, but the salary and benefits are so enticing that you wonder if maybe it's fate-perhaps a door swung open by the universe. Suddenly, you spot Arizona license plates splattered across your city. You notice cactus figurines and desert art displayed at your local HomeGoods. You spot a greeting card with a funny roadrunner cartoon at your drugstore. There's a bumper sticker in front of you in the drive-thru line that reads "Go West!" And, then, while grabbing a turkey and avocado sandwich, you overhear two friends chirping about their upcoming trip to Sedona.

Is it a sign from beyond or is it a fantastically masterful bundle of nerves in your brainstem doing their job?

But, wait; there's more. Your RAS is constantly seeking information that validates what you passionately believe. It filters the world through the parameters you've given it, and, in the spirit of a self-fulfilling prophecy, your beliefs highlight and manipulate those parameters.

Put simply, if you think you're awkward or undesirable or unpopular amongst your colleagues or peers or potential love interests, you almost certainly will be. Or, at least, that'll be your experience. And, similarly, if you're constantly inundating your mind with news reports and melodramatic tales that shout yet another reason why humanity is on the edge of an apocalypse, you'll see evidence show up in every angle of your life that confirms that, too.

Here's a mildly hilarious example from my life. A few months ago, I spent a lazy Saturday in pajamas, splayed across my sofa, hanging out with old episodes of *Celebrity Ghost Stories*. There was Joan Rivers unpacking a hair-raising tale about moving into an NYC penthouse that was haunted by a voodoo priestess. Diane Ladd spilled her harrowing experience with the ghost of a desperate, whistle-blowing Martha Mitchell. And so on. I probably watched 10 episodes, if not more. It was a spookily indulgent afternoon and I enjoyed every guilty minute of it.

Except, as it happens, there were undesirable consequences.

That night, while tucking my daughter into bed, every sound outside of her bedroom window, every creak of the rocking chair and every shadow floating across the hallway jolted my senses and made the hairs on the back of my neck stand at attention. Hours later, after my husband had burrowed under our bed sheets, I dashed down the hallway, squealing-convinced that there was a strange and menacing presence on my trail.

I realize that paranormal enthusiasts might shout that my ghostly binge had invited a spirit or two into my home. And maybe so. But probably not. Science has a different idea-one that says I'd simply fed my brain a day-long buffet of frightening impressions that it was now searching to confirm. The bottom line is this: your brain really, really likes what it knows. And, chances are high that it might need to start knowing some things other than what it's currently knowing.

You feel me?

The quality of information you regularly consume changes the biochemistry of your body, too. A 2011 study revealed that consuming negative television content causes a "catastrophizing of personal worries." The negative emotional toll that's presented when people consume negative material via television, as compared to those who watched fun-loving or neutral material, showed an increase in both anxious and gloomy moods after only 14 minutes {47}. While staggering, it's easy to explain. Fear-mongering news reports activate the sympathetic nervous system, causing your body to release stressful surges of cortisol and adrenaline, potentially leading to anxiety, emotional exhaustion, depressive episodes, and insomnia. Even fatal diseases {48}.

Conversely, when you're flooded with good news and sunny images and the kinds of comeback stories that inspire standing ovations-like the widowed mom of five who found love again, the dog who rescued his owner from a blazing fire or the teenager who recovered from a suicide attempt and launched a far-reaching non-profit, your body is flooded with feel-good chemicals like dopamine, oxytocin and serotonin {49}. And your brain is given a bevy of uplifting content to play with, search for and build upon.

Which means your consumption of good news creates a win-win; a self-fulfilling prophecy of the abundantly prosperous kind. The shades are drawn back, and the sunlight pours in. New doors of opportunity fly open. Faith starts coursing through the doubt, no matter how long it's been there. Because your brain is being increasingly "tuned" into, and is, therefore, "seeing" more and more of the good you're feeding it.

There's no way around it: the media you consume-including the blogs and push notifications you subscribe to, the podcasts you listen to, the YouTube videos you binge-watch, the Instagram and TikTok topics you follow, the conversations you entertain, and the news you read and absorb-will steer your thoughts, which will then steer your emotions, which will then steer your decisions and your health and, ultimately, the entire storyline of your life.

So, if you want to become the most confident, energized, happy and liberated version of yourself, which I suspect you do, and if you wish to intelligently direct the future in your favor, feed your brain empowering and inspiring ideas, impressions and solutions, every single day.

This doesn't mean turning a blind eye to essential facts-like, say, the global pandemic you need to be vividly aware of in order to protect your family, the dangerous intersection you should avoid, the fatal recall on dog food or the discrimination happening down the hall at your office, etc. But you should also be intentional about giving your brain information that illuminates miracles, encourages connections, points you toward answers, and maybe even makes you want to pop the champagne on occasion.

Because your health, your happiness, the fulfillment of your wildest dreams, and, ultimately, your future absolutely depend upon it.

RADICAL EXERCISE:

LET'S MEET AGAIN IN 20 YEARS

"Ask me anything...anything at all."

Imagine it's 20 years in the future. You've lived lots of life in two decades. You've seen wonderful things and awful things. Leapt from milestones to unremarkable moments in time. Enjoyed delicious meals with friends and loved ones. Fell in love with new songs that eventually became old. Wept and doubled over in laughter.

You've watched the world change, from fashion trends to technological advancements you could've never predicted. You made plans-some that were realized in ways that exceeded your expectations, and others that fell flat or turned sideways.

You find yourself standing at the doorway of a dimly-lit, quiet room. The ceiling is low and the walls are an iridescent white. The scent of lavender drifts through the air. Soft music is playing from somewhere in the near distance. A winding trail of burning candles leads to a small table in a far corner.

You notice that there's someone seated at the table, alone. Then, to your surprise, you realize it's you-exactly 20 years from today. Except it's not just any version of you. It's a joyful, peaceful and optimal version of you-the one who carved a trail of wise, authentic and empowered decisions between today and then.

The one who finally, self-determinedly stopped dancing with the ghosts of the past. But also the one who began to recognize the gifts in pain. The one who stopped overthinking and started moving in the direction of her dreams, even when she didn't know what she was doing. The one who forgave herself and others, but who also held the discernment to know when it was time to speak up, and draw a line in the sand, and move on.

The one who grew so tired of people-pleasing, she lost interest. The one who, instead, grew deliciously fond of pleasing herself, so long as it never meant dishonoring or violating someone else.

The one who met her reflection in the mirror each morning with compassion, courage, responsibility and tenderness. The one who drifted to dreams each night with a spirit of acceptance, integrity and grace. Even when she hadn't shown up as her best self that day.

Upon recognizing you, her face lights up with excitement and gladness. She launches from her seat and motions you toward her. "Come, come! I've been waiting for you!" she exclaims.

The two of you rush to embrace. It's the most cherished and safe you've felt in a long time. She clasps your hands and gives them a loving squeeze, and asks that you take a seat. "I'm so happy to see you. I'm so proud of you. Thank you," she gushes. "Ask me anything... anything at all!"

Her eyes sparkle with affection, as though you're a child that she adores unconditionally, but also as though you're her hero. You're the one whose brave and honest decisions gave her the wonderful life she's living.

So, go ahead and ask her anything. Anything at all. Then, close your eyes, take a deep breath and listen. Because you know that everything she says is true, and rooted in love, and aligned with your highest good.

She knows your darkest secrets-including the things you've never been able to confess to anyone. She knows every dream that, up until this moment, you've yet to realize. Also the ones you've yet to surrender, but maybe need to. She knows your anxious tics, hang-ups and patterns, and understands all of your most buried pain points, but she also knows all of your next right beginnings, endings... and moves.

She's your sacred text in human form-the one that holds the answers you seek.

What are they?

LET'S MEET AGAIN IN 20 YEARS

THINGS I NEED TO KNOW TODAY, FOR THE EMPOWERED FUTURE I'M IN PROCESS OF CREATING:

CUSTOM-DESIGN YOUR ABUNDANCE BLUEPRINT

Gone are the days of sketching plans that keep you shy and playing small.

We've almost arrived at the celebratory toast. If you were to view this process in terms of a home renovation, this is the part where you'd be putting the final coats of paint on the walls, selecting art to hang and floral centerpieces to set. You'd be getting ready to celebrate the results of your labor. But, in this program, I'm not after a grand finale. Instead, I want you to exit this experience having built a sparkling vision for your life-one that's customized to the truest, most unsullied desires of your soul. One you're fizzing with excitement to realize and expand upon. One your future self will be so grateful for. In other words, I don't want this journey to end here.

As this curtain draws to a close, this is the part where I ask you to make a vow to yourself to stop playing small, and to start being brave and honest about what you really, really want. Not what the faulty messages from your early childhood programming say you want. Not what your deepest insecurities say you want. Not what your overbearing parent or pushy partner says you should want. But, what you believe is somehow mandated for you-the eternal you, underneath all of the noise of familial expectation and societal pressure and subliminal shame.

We're all sort of hunting for the golden answer to a more abundant life, aren't we? The human plight is one of scavenging for happiness, meaning, success and validation, however one defines it. But, what if the secret to an extraordinary life is soberingly less elusive and exhilarating than one might assume? What if it involves designing a clear and intentional blueprint-one that begins with slowing down and having courageous conversations with yourself? One that's designed to mirror your essence and individuality?

Remember what I said about taking radical responsibility for the life that you've been given? This is where I want you to step onto that throne of authority and reclaim you power. This is your story and no one gets to live inside of it but you.

But, know this: building an abundance blueprint isn't about seeking immunization from being human. That's not possible, no matter how much fame, money or genetic advantage you've got. There's no indelible escape from the harsh whims of mother nature or relational misunderstandings or angsty drivers slamming on their brakes in traffic.

Life happens. Bad days happen. Conflicts happen. For God's sake, global pandemics happen. And, ultimately, change and pain are inevitable. So long as you have breath, there's no side door offering respite from disappointment, loneliness or loss.

With the previous exercise in mind, and the guidance drawn from it, I want you to thoughtfully design a blueprint for how you're going to show up in the world as the engineer and authoritarian of your own happiness, no matter what might storm over your plans. This is about deciding how you're going to contribute to the human story, for however much time you've got left to play a role in it. It's deciding how you're going to honor the future self that you just visited.

So, before we begin, I ask that you recall the specific pain point(s) that begged you to buy this book. Whether it was to anchor the confidence to build your business idea so that you can ditch your soul-sucking job and segue into financial freedom, or end the parasitic relationship and move across the coast for a badly-needed fresh start, choose the most urgent goals (ideally one or two, but no more than three). Choose ones that send anticipation and splendor whirring through your bloodstream.

Give your plan a timescale that's achievable, but within your field of vision. Six months is generally ideal, as it'll feel close enough that you'll be able to tap into momentum, but will also give you ample time to radically transform your reality. When I changed my life a decade ago, I made head-spinning strides in only six months.

And, all the while, know this: I'm chanting for your prosperity and am applauding the courageous work you've done so far. I'm already jazzed to hear about all of the ways you've wowed yourself. Here's to your more empowered future-the one you've dreamt and prayed and wept about for a long, long time. The one you consciously constructed and designed. You, not anyone else.

1. Get radically clear about what's not working.

The overpriced seminars that preyed upon your emotions and further drained your precious finances. The strategies that fell on deaf ears. The collaborations that combusted in a puff of smoke. The romantic decisions that scathed you dozens of times. The things that seemed too good to be true...and were. Maybe some things that you ultimately came to realize were never deserving of your love or friendship or late hours to begin with. Perhaps the ways you failed to show compassion, fairness or respect to others.

Search for the common denominators and themes within the choices that corroded your bank account or caused you disappointment and grief.

Returning to the first chapter of this book, consider some questions: Were these circumstances driven by a nasty core belief about your yourself? Were they an attempt to appease someone? Were they made on impulse? Did you open yourself up to bad advice from a foolish source? This reflection isn't to torture you, but to make space for clarity so that you don't wander into the same dead-end outcomes again.

2. Spotlight every decision that worked in your favor.

The interview question you answered swimmingly. The app you downloaded that helped you organize your bills. The life-unlocking webinar or therapy session that smacked you with one "ah ha!" after another. Or, perhaps, the logo designer who brought your brand to life. Again, see if there are any common denominators and themes blinking at you, pointing you toward a wiser decision-making process and strategy.

3. Decide how you want your life to feel, day to day.

This holds the magic key to joy and fulfillment, and will eliminate noise you didn't know was driving you insane or causing you unnecessary micro-stresses. So often we draft elaborate, life-altering plans that are based upon a series of ideals that were woven into our paradigm years or decades ago.

We might be oblivious to how miserable we've become trying to align with something we don't love. We might think something is a "want" when it's really a "should." So, in an effort to sidestep those ideals and access your truth, here are some questions to ask yourself (among others that they might inspire):

- *Am I motivated by a need to feel independent and free, or do I appreciate the coziness and security of accountability and teamwork?*

- *Do I crave the whimsical rush of creativity and variety, or the ease of organization and predictability? Perhaps a calm and intimate feel, or an energized, thumping rhythm?*

- *Am I happiest with anonymity and privacy, or do I contribute the most when I feel seen and known?*

- *Am I drawn to a bustling metropolis, a tightly-knit suburban community or a breezy countryside?*

- *Do I want a spouse/children/a closet packed full of designer labels/an advanced degree, etc. because I'm trying to win over someone's admiration, or am I so on fire for this dream that I'm willing to make uncomfortable sacrifices in order to realize it?*

These types of questions are the fundamentals to building a life you love. So, before you sketch another plan, get clear about how you want to feel, day to day. This'll point you toward so many of your next right decisions-from career to personal fulfillment.

4. Take an honest audit of your personal and professional relationships.

Yes, even the ones you're trying so hard not to know are poisoning you. This is essential. A brilliant study conducted by Harvard researcher and psychologist, Dr. David McClelland, determined that 95 percent of your success-or failure-in life is directly linked to the people you bump elbows with on a regular basis {50}. That's right. The phone calls you take, the invitations you accept and the people you welcome into your celebrations and milestones have a massive impact on how you feel about yourself. This also shapes how you show up in the world and how you're perceived by the people you most hope to impress.

Scary, huh? Also exciting, especially when you realize that this might be the piece that's been holding you hostage.

Here are some questions to ask yourself:

- *Do this person enhance my happiness or dampen it?*

- *Does this person clap when I shine, or have I noticed that they tend to get weird and vanish until the excitement settles?*

- *Does their affection run hot and cold-perhaps depending upon how much I'm feeding their agendas, pacifying their troubles or satisfying their demands?*

- *Do I leave our conversations and hang-outs feeling inspired and recharged, or do I often feel as though the life force has been siphoned out of me?*

- *Have I been a generous friend to them, or have I been neglectful, one-sided or selfish?*

- *Who am I missing from my life, yet crave? Coaches, mentors, study partners, mom friends, muses or kindred spirits? Perhaps a lover who'll cherish my wit and quirks?*

Stop feeling guilty if you need to show some relationships the exit door. In a world of regurgitated mantras like, "True friends stick by your side no matter what," I passionately disagree. Relationship dynamics are nuanced and multi-faceted, and necessary goodbyes will never make you a bad person. There are few decisions more destructive to your life than being a prisoner to an expired relationship.

So, nix the second-guessing and shame about the goodbyes you need to make. Your mother didn't haul you around in her womb for nine months for you to spend your precious months and years entrapping yourself in ambivalent, energy-draining or miserable exchanges. You owe yourself an enlivening community.

There's a quantum physics principle that says when we emotionally, mentally and physically bond with someone over time, we become energetically entangled {51} with them. This might explain why some endings feel like ripping flesh from flesh. You might feel like your very heart is being yanked from your body. Understand that, if so, this intense feeling doesn't necessarily mean that the relationship is "meant to be." Maybe it does, but very likely it doesn't. Only you know what gives you joy and life and peace, and what steals it all from you.

Regardless, this concept offers further incentive to more consciously create your social circle. If you're feeling frustrated and lost in this realm (hand wagging high; I've been there!), I beg you to grab a copy of Lori Harder's book, *A Tribe Called Bliss*. She'll have you thundering with epiphany about the friendships that have been giving you pause, and point you in the direction of those that'll make your soul feel right at home.

5. Decide and declare, in vibrant detail, the person you desire to become.

Who is she? Who is this amazing person who has everything you crave out of life?

Step into the movie she's living. Walk around inside of it and explore. Then, pull the movie from inside of your head and get the frames onto the page. Describe what you hear and feel and see, in vivid detail. What is she wearing? Who is she chatting with? What's the first thing she does in the morning? Revisit your responses in previous chapters, where you explored your long-held fantasies and dreams.

Let's say, for example, you long to purchase a house on a hill in the neighborhood of your dreams. You could see yourself being handed the keys to your new abode. You could see yourself planting a sunflower garden in your backyard, elbow-deep in the soil, or cozying into your reading nook with a rapturous novel and a warm mug of hot chocolate. Or, perhaps, standing in your crisp, white, sun-washed kitchen, grinding coffee beans in your bathrobe and fuzzy slippers.

You might see yourself signing the contracts and depositing the checks. Exchanging the vows and zipping up your suitcase for a Caribbean honeymoon. Rescuing the puppies and having their collars engraved with your email and phone number. Renting a cabin in the mountains to put the final touches on your book or business plan. It's all about you, baby. Just get clear about who this person is.

Wander into the wisest corners of your mind and follow her around for an entire day. Memorize her habits and conversations. This person wants and needs you as much as you want to become her.

6. Once you've imagined the end result, slowly move in reverse.

Now that you've visualized the future you desire, and have held a clear snapshot of it in your mind, slowly move in reverse to where you are now, "unpacking" the specific action steps that guided you straight to your destination. This holds the answers that you may already know, but don't know that you know.

What are you going to do, beginning now, to move into this desired future, whatever it is? Purchase the domain name and secure the LLC? Eliminate the subscriptions and open a savings account? End the nightmarish relationship and secure a patient, warm-natured therapist so that you can work on becoming the version of yourself that's healthy and primed for a lasting, fulfilling commitment? Flesh out what you "see" and organize the frames into clear, actionable steps.

7. Commit to your plan and toast to its motion.

One of the most powerful steps you can ever take is to decide. I don't mean halfway decide, or loosely decide, but *really* decide that you deserve an abundant, fulfilling and rewarding life experience, and are already in the process of realizing whatever that means for you. You deserve it, yes, even after everything that happened. Yes, despite how many times you've procrastinated or quit or screwed up.

Your precious blueprint is about to be set in motion and you must toss it out into the world in faith. No holding back this time. Celebrate its creation. Reread and visualize its luxurious components, lit up in all of its custom-designed glory. Let it live in your closest thoughts at all times. Believe in its power. Feel the buzz of progress. Know that you deserve it. Because you do.

Dream with courage and intention, like your life depends upon it. Because it does.

CUSTOM-DESIGNING MY ABUNDANCE BLUEPRINT:

1 - HERE'S CLARITY ABOUT THE ACTIONS AND EFFORTS THAT DIDN'T WORK OUT SO WELL:

CUSTOM-DESIGNING MY ABUNDANCE BLUEPRINT:

2 - HERE'S A SPOTLIGHT OVER MY BEST DECISIONS, AND THE ACTIONS THAT'VE WORKED IN MY FAVOR:

CUSTOM-DESIGNING MY ABUNDANCE BLUEPRINT:

3 - AND HERE'S HOW I WANT
MY LIFE TO FEEL, DAY TO DAY, GOING FORWARD:

CUSTOM-DESIGNING MY ABUNDANCE BLUEPRINT:

4A - HERE'S AN HONEST AUDIT, GOOD AND BAD, OF MY CURRENT RELATIONSHIPS:

CUSTOM-DESIGNING MY ABUNDANCE BLUEPRINT:

4B - ...AND HERE ARE THE KINDS OF CONNECTIONS
I INTEND TO ATTRACT INTO MY LIFE:

CUSTOM-DESIGNING MY ABUNDANCE BLUEPRINT:

5A - HERE'S A DESCRIPTION OF THE PERSON I'M BECOMING: HER APPEARANCE, CONVERSATIONS, HABITS, HOME AND STYLE...

CUSTOM-DESIGNING MY ABUNDANCE BLUEPRINT:

5B - ...AND HERE'S A VIVID DESCRIPTION OF THE EMOTIONS I FEEL WHEN I IMAGINE WALKING AROUND IN HER SHOES:

THESE ARE THE SMALL BUT SMART ACTION STEPS I'LL BEGIN TAKING RIGHT NOW, TO MOVE IN THE DIRECTION OF MY DESIRED LIFE:

- ☐

- ☐

- ☐

- ☐

- ☐

- ☐

- ☐

...AND THESE ARE THE SUPER GUTSY ACTIONS I'LL TAKE BETWEEN NOW AND MY TARGET DATE, BECAUSE I WON'T LET FEAR RUN THE SHOW ANYMORE:

☐

☐

☐

☐

☐

☐

☐

MY CUSTOM-DESIGNED ABUNDANCE BLUEPRINT

HERE'S A SNAPSHOT OF MY FUTURE, FOR DAILY REFERENCE:

SIGNED, SEALED & SET IN MOTION ON:

PHASE FOUR

MY MOST POWERFUL REVELATIONS
DURING THIS PHASE HAVE BEEN...

PHASE FOUR

RADICAL DAILY 4 CHECK-IN:

ANY MEMORABLE GIFTS
YOU'VE GIVEN TO YOURSELF LATELY?

A CLOSING INVITATION...

I DARE YOU TO PROSPER.

I DARE YOU TO NOT MERELY STAND IN THE SHADOWED PARKS OF WHAT IS MOST FAMILIAR, ADMIRING YOUR CITY OF LIGHTS FROM A DISTANCE, BUT TO BUILD A BRIDGE AND MEET YOUR DREAMS WHERE THEY ARE REALIZED.

I DARE YOU TO BE UNCOMFORTABLE, AND TO BE REFINED BY THE RED-HOT FLAMES OF THAT DISCOMFORT.

I DARE YOU TO FOLLOW THE VOICE OF YOUR INSTINCTS, AND TO BE LED BY THE FRAGRANCE OF YOUR HEART'S DESIRE. I DARE YOU TO REACH, WITH A MIGHTY FIST, INTO THE ETHER, AND PULL EVERY DREAM INTO THE CONSTRUCTS OF YOUR REALITY.

I DARE YOUR WISHES AND BELIEFS TO ALIGN.

I DARE YOU TO GET IT RIGHT THIS TIME.

annnnnd...you did it!
(Epilogue)

Congratulations, world-changer. Welcome to your renovation–one that's only just begun.

Here's a quick piece of awesome news: research in neuroscience shows that, on average, it takes around 66 days for new habits to crystallize on a cellular level {53}, which means that, if you've followed the eight-week format with an open heart and a determined mind, and consistently shown up for the Radical Daily 4, you've nearly reached the threshold of transformation.

The journey of redesigning your life doesn't end here, though. Or ever. This program is meant to be a radical wake-up call within your personal evolution. So, as you progress in your mindset and pursuits, I invite you to return to this material, perhaps yearly. I return to it seasonally! Because each time you swing open its doors, you'll be stepping into it with fresh eyes. Which means the takeaways will be different–landing in places they might not have landed before, lighting up possibilities that you once weren't ready to see.

So, as we part ways for now but definitely not forever, I want to leave you with something.

Not long ago, I interviewed Dr. Edith Eger for a magazine story, as I mentioned in this book's introduction. In case you don't feel like shuffling back 100 or so pages, she's a Holocaust survivor who became a renowned psychologist, going on to author two *New York Times* bestsellers and being featured on *Super Soul Sunday.* We had a magnificent conversation about human resilience and the power of choice, pausing several times to fight back tears and affirm each other's journeys. She nearly took my breath away.

To grasp the power of this, let me remind you that I've been lucky to interview lots of celebrated people over the years. Galley copies of highly-anticipated books land in my mailbox regularly, so it's rare for a body of work to captivate me anymore. But Dr. Eger's book, *The Gift*, had become a fixture on my nightstand for months prior–serving as my companion through the disorienting aftermath of a traumatizing brush with death. Her compassionate wisdom had braided itself into my psyche, providing so much fortification.

(cont.) Epilogue

As my conversation with Dr. Eger was drawn to a close, I remembered something a customer had said to me once, years prior, during my days as a traveling makeup artist.

When I'd asked her what kind of look she wanted me to create for her that day, she'd grinned devilishly and said, "Oh, honey, I'm up for anything. I got out of a bad marriage last year. I just traveled abroad for the first in my life. I'm finally becoming the woman I always wanted to be." After a pause, she added, "You'll get there one day..."

When I said goodbye to Dr. Eger, tapped my recorder button and saved the audio file to my computer, it hit me: I'd finally become the woman I'd dreamt of becoming for so long.

That's not to say that there aren't so many other ways I wish to evolve and stretch out. Truth be told, I've got a catalogue of shortcomings I wish to improve upon, and a world of other things I plan to birth, should life grant me the luxury of time.

Let's keep these lights turned on.

Stroll over to laceyjohnson.com for more energizing kinship, sparkling conversations and empowering research.

@thelaceyjohnson

f t

But, no matter what happens next, here I am. Right now. Gone are the days of romanticizing the version of myself that once seemed so far away and elusive. She isn't a figment of my dreams anymore; I'm standing in her shoes. I'm moving to the melody of her song. I'm carrying out her plans and aspirations. And, though the reality might not feel quite as chic or glamorous as the dream once did, and certainly isn't without snags, it's so potently fulfilling. I know I'm exactly where I'm supposed to be.

Which brings me back to you.

You know that person you've always fantasized about becoming? Here you are. You know that life you've long dreamt about? It's not whistling around the corner or seducing you from a distant universe; it's right here, at your doorstep. Your possibilities have arrived. Which is also to say that I hope you'll have the courage, the determination, the faith and the self-belief to step into it, all the way, and live it...

Sources:

1 - *OPRAH DAILY:* "IS IT HEALTHY TO BE A HOPELESS ROMANTIC?"

2 - BRUCELIPTON.COM: "HAPPY,HEALTHY CHILD: A HOLISTIC APPROACH"

3 - *SCIENCE DAILY*

4 - CENTER ON THE DEVELOPING CHILD, HARVARD UNIVERSITY

5- WORLDOMETER

6 - *THE EAST SIDER*

7 - *PSYCHOLOGY TODAY*

8 - *PSYCH PEDIA*

9 - *OPRAH DAILY:* "SUSPECT A FRIEND IS JEALOUS OF YOU? HERE'S WHAT TO DO"

10 - UNIVERSITY OF MINNESOTA

11 - *PSYCHOLOGY TODAY*

12 - *THE JOURNAL OF PERSONALITY AND SOCIAL PSYCHOLOGY*

13 - ORLANDO HEALTH

14 - AMERICAN PSYCHOLOGICAL ASSOCIATION

15 - *HOW TO LIVE A GOOD LIFE*

16 - *THE TELEGRAPH*

17 - *YOUGOVAMERICA*

18 - *ENTREPRENEUR*

19 - *FORBES*

20 - *THE CONNECT MAGAZINE:* "THE ANTHEM OF GIGI BUTLER"

21 - *CBS*

22 - *OPRAH DAILY:* "12 TECHNIQUES TO START YOUR JOURNEY TO SELF-DISCOVERY"

23 - *BBC*

24 - *NEWCASTLE HERALD*

25 - *BRITANNICA*

26 - *THE UNDEFEATED*

27 - *IMBD*

28 - *NEWSWEEK*

29 - *LA TIMES*

30 - *UCLA NEWSROOM*

31 - *HRSA*

32 - ANNUAL REVIEW OF PSYCHOLOGY: *"...EMPATHY AND MIRROR NEURONS"*

33 - ROLLING STONE; "JESSICA SIMPSON: PORTRAIT OF A LIVING DOLL"

34 - *BILLBOARD*

35 - *THE CONNECT*: "SPIRITUAL MASTERMIND DEEPAK CHOPRA ON HOW TO CREATE AN EXTRAORDINARY WORLD"

36 - *YOU ARE THE UNIVERSE*

37 - SCIENCEDIRECT

38 - *POPSUGAR*: "DEPRESSION AND ANXIETY ARE ON THE RISE IN YOUNG PEOPLE, BUT IS SOCIAL MEDIA TO BLAME?'

39 - CLEVELAND CLINIC

40 - TALKSPACE

41 - *MINDING THE MENTAL MESS*

42 - *OPRAH DAILY;* "HOW TO INCREASE INTIMACY IN YOUR RELATIONSHIP:

43 - MICHIGAN STATE UNIVERSITY: THE KEY TO SUCCESS IS FAILURE

44 - *THE TOP FIVE REGRETS OF THE DYING: A LIFE TRANSFORMED BY THE DEARLY DEPARTING*

45 - *THE CONNECT MAGAZINE*: "'SHARK TANK' CONTENDER DAYMOND JOHN GETS CANDID ABOUT HIS PRIVATE MOMENTS TO THE TOP"

46 - *RISE AND GRIND*

47 - THE BRITISH PSYCHOLOGICAL SOCIETY: THE PSYCHOLOGICAL IMPACT OF NEGATIVE TV NEWS BULLETINS

48 - *ABC NEWS*: YOU REALLY CAN BE SCARED TO DEATH

49 - *CEREBRUM*: WHY INSPIRING STORIES MAKE US REACT; THE NEUROSCIENCE OF NARRATIVE

50 - *THE COMPOUND EFFECT*

51 - *THE POSSIBILITY PRINCIPLE*

52 - *EUROPEAN JOURNAL OF SOCIAL PSYCHOLOGY: HOW ARE HABITS FORMED*

"RUN TOWARD YOUR DREAMS LIKE YOUR LIFE IS CATCHING FIRE. BECAUSE, WHETHER OR NOT YOU CAN SMELL IT BURNING, IT IS."

- LACEY JOHNSON, RADICAL LIFE RENOVATION